IMPROVING JUVENILE JUSTICE

IMPROVING JUVENILE JUSTICE
Power Advocacy, Diversion, Decriminaliza-
tion, Deinstitutionalization, and Due Process

Harjit S. Sandhu, M.A., M.S.W., Ph.D.
Oklahoma State University,
Stillwater, Oklahoma

C. Wayne Heasley, M.S., J.D.
Washburn University of Topeka,
Topeka, Kansas

1981

HV
9104
.S3154
West

 **HUMAN SCIENCES PRESS**
72 Fifth Avenue   3 Henrietta Street
NEW YORK, NY 10011 ● LONDON, WC2E 8LU

Printed in the United States of America
123456789   987654321

Library of Congress Cataloging in Publication Data

Sandhu, Harjit S.

  Improving juvenile justice.

  Includes index.
  1. Juvenile justice, Administration of—United States.   I. Heasley, C. Wayne, joint
author.   II. Title.
HV9104.S3154   364.3'6'0973   LC80-36813
ISBN 0-89885-033-9
ISBN 0-89885-044-4 (pbk.)

WE AFFECTIONATELY DEDICATE THIS
WORK TO OUR PARENTS

Charles D. Heasley
and
Mary E. Heasley
of
Charlotte, North Carolina

Lall S. Sandhu
and
Gurkirpal K. Sandhu
of
Jullundur, India

CONTENTS

LIST OF TABLES AND FIGURES

Tables

Figures

FOREWORD

Concern with disruptive, delinquent, and/or predatory and violent behavior of youth is prevalent throughout the United States as well as in several other industrialized and post-industrialized countries. Societal response to the criminal and non-criminal misbehavior of youth has been an area of great interest for more than a century. However, despite considerable legislative and judicial action at the state and federal levels and billions of dollars in intervention programs, the problem has not abated. In fact, some assert that it is more serious today than it has been in the past. Public concern appears to focus on how youth can be controlled so that their behavior will not offend or interfere with the dominant adult society. Because social policies and youth programs reflect greater concern for coercive social control than for enhancing youth socialization for adult roles, many have observed that this society appears to "dislike" children and youth.

Within the past decade several states have passed extremely punitive laws governing juvenile law violations. In fact, in many instances juveniles are being dealt with far more stringently than are adults who commit similar crimes. These actions have been taken despite a decline in the youth population and in juvenile crime. Moreover, the situation is aggravated by the fact that youth are increasingly being denied access to legitimate adult roles in employment and community affairs.

On the basis of the concept parens patriae the juvenile court has been authorized to intervene wherever a juvenile's behavior is deemed problematic for the family, society or even the youth. This misbehavior which includes truancy, running away, incorrigibility, and unruliness has been as sufficient a basis for adjudication and incarceration as was the commission of a serious felony. With the passage of the Juvenile Justice and Delinquency Prevention Act, a remedy was available to states to develop other alternatives to justice system processing. Some states have moved far toward achievement of that goal, but others have delayed and not modified their archaic codes and structures. But, even where alternatives have been developed, there also has been a tendency to "widen the net" of social control by bringing more and more youth under official surveillance. Recent data indicate that as of 1977, 46 youth per thousand youth population were processed by the juvenile court in that year—making the United States one of the most control-oriented societies in the world. It is also particularly unfortunate that juveniles from poor neighborhoods, minority groups and single-parent households are more likely to be apprehended; whereas for the middle class voluntary community services are provided for youth who are charged with less serious delinquency.

Sandhu and Heasley offer much food for thought and action in their critique of the existing juvenile justice systems and in their proposals for policy and program alternatives. Their identification of decriminalization, deinstitutionalization, and diversion as key action concepts provided a framework for their critique and led to their development of "power advocacy" as a general intervention strategy. They argue that communities must take positive proactive steps to improve programs for youth socialization and maturation. But, if communities are to deploy power advocacy successfully, they must develop appropriate social structures for effective prevention, treatment and control programs. In the past decade federal grants have stimulated the development of local initiatives for juvenile programs. However, these approaches often lacked coherence and were developed in an ad hoc manner. They call attention to the political aspects of delinquency prevention and control, but they also emphasize the vested interests of professionals as a constraint on service delivery.

This examination of diversion alternatives is one of the more thorough in the literature today and should be of particular value to practitioners because the authors analyze a broad range of alternative programs and provide specific recommendations for the initiation and implementation of these types of programs. They emphasize the need for honest and genuine reform, not just symbolic gestures that only serve to maintain traditions and the status quo.

In recent years the United States has moved toward increased formalization of the juvenile justice system, ostensibly to enhance due process and the protection of civil liberties. These approaches seem to have benefitted serious juvenile offenders far more than minor and status offenders who are often dealt with punitively with little regard for their individual rights. In contrast to the U.S., changes in many European countries, Australia and Canada have moved in the opposite direction. They have adopted more informal approaches with milder sanctions. Through the development of social mechanisms outside the court, lay persons in the community as well as human service professionals have assumed more critical responsibilities in decision making.

This volume should be of great benefit to administrators and other practitioners interested in serving troubled youth more effectively. It provides a perspective about youth and juvenile justice, and also a series of recommendations for achieving the goals that one seeks.

ROSEMARY C. SARRI
National Assessment of Juvenile Corrections
University of Michigan

PREFACE

In recent years, the juvenile justice system in the United States has, with justification, been subjected to harsh criticism by youth advocates, victims of youth crime, youths, parents, and politicians. Unfortunately, the effectuation of change in juvenile justice has been a slow and difficult process because of, inter alia, the pervasive statutory base of the juvenile justice system, the enormous power and discretion of juvenile court judges, and the almost complete lack of demand for accountability.

The authors have identified major problems in juvenile justice, described strategies being employed to deal with these problems, and proposed actions which, the authors believe, are necessary to respond to these problems more effectively.

Decriminalization, diversion, deinstitutionalization, and due process are topics given extensive coverage. In addition, a detailed explanation of "power advocacy" is presented as a vehicle which residents of a locality served by a juvenile court can utilize to develop the capability to expeditiously eliminate, modify, merge, expand, create, monitor, evaluate, and investigate delinquency prevention and control policies, programs, and practices. In the final chapter, the authors proffer recommendations for the juvenile court and the agencies and organizations with which the juvenile court must interact to fulfill its mission.

The authors wish to express special gratitude to Mrs. Sarah Ann Heasley for typing, editing and performing other manuscript-related tasks; and to Mrs. Roop Sandhu for literature search, proofreading and index-preparation. The first author also wants to acknowledge the help rendered by several librarians, notable of whom are John Phillips, Vicki Phillips, Edward Hollman, Thomas Storek, Terry Basford, and Mary Brown.

THE AUTHORS

Outline for Chapter 1

Juvenile Justice: An Overreaction

Breadth of the Court's Jurisdiction
Juvenile Laws and Delinquency Control Agencies: An Historical
Review
    Children as Laborers
    Indenturing of Children
    Confining Children in Institutions
    Placement in Free Foster Homes
    Reforming and Child Saving
    Diverse Theories of Delinquency Causation
    Federal Involvement
Historical Consequences for Children
    Deteriorating Family Government
    Crumbling Social Order
    Damaging Urban Life
    Child-Saving Movement
    Parent-Child Relations
Juvenile Justice: A Case of Over-Criminalization, Over-
Processing, Over-Incarceration, Denial of Due Process Protec-
tions and Lack of Demand for Accountability
    Over-Criminalization
    Over-Processing
    Over-Incarceration
    Denial of Due Process Protections
    Lack of Demand for Accountability

Chapter 1

JUVENILE JUSTICE

An Overreaction

Breadth of the Court's Jurisdiction

The first impression one gathers when studying juvenile justice is that lawmakers, police, courts, and juvenile correction officers *overreact* against youth. A major reason for this overreaction is the broad jurisdiction of the juvenile court. Offenses for which children come under the jurisdiction of the juvenile court include both acts which are considered crimes if committed by adults and status offenses. Status offender statutes allow children to be processed for running away from home, truanting from school, violating curfew restrictions, indulging in sexually promiscuous activities, possessing alcoholic beverages, and the like. Status offenses also include such vague terms as incorrigibility, waywardness, and "beyond control."

The juvenile court also has jurisdiction over youths who are without proper parental care or control, subsistence, or education as required by law, or other care or control necessary for their physical, mental, or emotional health, or who have been placed for care or adoption in violation of law, or who have been abandoned, or physically, mentally, emotionally, or sexually abused by their parents, custodians, or guardians, or who are without a parent, custodian, or guardian. Juvenile statutes may classify these youths as "dependent," "neglected," or "deprived."

JUVENILE LAWS AND DELINQUENCY CONTROL AGENCIES: AN HISTORICAL REVIEW

Children as Laborers

To understand the evolution of juvenile laws and delinquency control agencies, we must begin with the period during which slave owners used slave children merely to further their own ends and proceed to the feudal system in Europe where the worth of children was determined by what they could contribute to the feudal lord. During slavery and the days of feudalism, children's individual needs, capacities, purposes, or plans were not recognized. Later, the 43rd Act of Queen Elizabeth (1601) provided that children be set to work at "flax, hemp, wood" etc., under the supervision of overseers. Under this act, children were placed under apprenticeship or farmed out to work for others. If children were unable to work, they were placed in a "poor house." If they were unwilling to work, they were punished. These practices traveled to America along with the immigrants.

Indenturing of Children

To fully utilize the capacity of children's labor, all the American colonies indentured children. Unattached, unsupported, and neglected children were assigned to a person or a family who agreed to be responsible for them. These children were required to perform a certain amount of work prior to the expiration of their term of indenture.

Confining Children in Institutions

Disobedience on the part of children was a serious offense for which children could be sent to jail and even whipped. In 1819, Illinois passed a law providing for the punishment of disobedient children.[1]

> "An Act Respecting Crimes and Punishments" Approved March 23, 1819, Laws of Illinois, 1819.
> Section 10. *Disobedience of Children and Servants.*—Be it further enacted, that if any children or servants shall, contrary to the obedience due to their parents or masters, resist or refuse to obey their lawful commands, upon complaint thereof to any justice of the peace, it shall be lawful for such justice of the peace to send him or them so offending to jail or house of correction, there to remain until they shall humble themselves to the said parents' or masters' satisfaction . . .

Around 1824–25, an era of institutions began in America. J. V. N. Yates, Secretary of State for New York, advocated the establishment of almshouses for neglected and dependent children. Yates thought these children could be given some instruction and moral training before they were indentured.

In 1825, the first House of Refuge was opened in New York City for both delinquent boys and girls. Shortly thereafter, two other such schools were established in Boston and Philadelphia. Children in Houses of Refuge were apprenticed when they were considered ready for release. Managers of Refuge Houses employed very repressive treatment and harsh discipline. Abuses in the operation of almshouses resulted in thousands of dependent children being removed from them and being placed in families, orphan asylums, reformatories, and other institutions.[2]

Placement in Free Foster Homes

In 1851, Charles Loring Brace founded the New York Childrens Aid Society. His influence was felt nationwide. With the help of these societies, Brace placed children in free foster homes. Many of these children were shipped from eastern states hundreds of miles away to western frontier states. Boys worked on new farms, whereas girls worked in homes. At this point, interest was shifting from the institution back to the family. A warm parent–child relationship was recognized as an essential ingredient in building good character.

Reforming and Child Saving

The period between 1870 to 1900 has been called an era of reformation and a child-saving movement. Chicago became the scene of action for what we call today the child-saving movement. Chicago child savers led by influential women's groups sought the help of the Chicago Bar Association to draft the first juvenile court laws. Writers were discovering the restless spirit of adolescence and the special youth problems associated with adolescence. Julia Addams blamed the large city life for many of the problems of youth and their families. The reformers wanted to remove juveniles from the criminal court and deal with them in separate juvenile courts which could give special attention to youth problems. The efforts of child savers came to fruition when the first juvenile court law was enacted in Illinois in 1899. The Illinois law was enthusiastically received and duplicated by many other states. Using the doctrine of *Parens Patriae*, the juvenile court sought to act as the "father of the children" under its jurisdiction. Under the pretense of protection of children, these new laws also extended the court's jurisdiction to deal with cases of incorrigibility, neglect, and dependency. Although one of the rationales for creation of the juvenile court was to decriminalize youths by removing them from criminal courts, laws which established juvenile courts actually resulted in the criminalization of much youth behavior which had theretofore been noncriminal. Following is an excerpt from the Illinois Juvenile Court Act, 1899, which documents the wide powers given to the juvenile court under the first Juvenile Court Act.[3]

The First Juvenile Court Act

"An Act to Regulate the Treatment and Control of Dependent Neglected and Delinquent Children," Laws of Illinois, 1899.
    This act shall apply only to children under the age of 16 years.
. . . For the purposes of this act the words dependent child shall mean any child who for any reason is destitute or homeless or abandoned; or dependent upon the public for support; or has not proper parental care or guardianship or who habitually begs or receives alms; or who is found living in any house of ill fame or with any vicious or disreputable person; or whose home, by reason of neglect, cruelty or depravity on the part of its parents, guardian or other person in whose care it may be, is an unfit place for such a child; and any child under the age of 8 years who is found peddling or selling any article or singing or playing any musical instrument upon the streets or giving any public entertainment. The words delinquent child shall include any child under the age of 16 years who violates any law of this State or any city or village ordinance. . .

It should be noted that during most of the 19th century, reformers and lawmakers seemed to hold the *individual* responsible for his delinquency. Toward the end of the century, there was some recognition that social conditions prevailing in certain areas may be responsible for high delinquency rates. To alleviate conditions in the areas and neighborhoods affected by delinquency, some isolated efforts were made to set up settlement houses, and neighborhood and area projects. The outstanding examples are those of Hull House, founded by Jane Addams in 1889, and the Chicago Area Project later started by Clifford R. Shaw in 1932. The Hull House provided children with educational, vocational, and recreational opportunities. The Chicago Area Project was more of a community-based project involving area leaders in reintegrating youth into the community.[4]

Diverse Theories of Delinquency Causation

During the 20th century, professionals from diverse disciplines promulgated various theories of delinquency causation, with some theoretical and others empirically based. The phrenologists led by Lombroso, an Italian medical doctor, thought that criminals and delinquents were born. Sheldon looked at them as mesomorphs. Somewhat similar to Lombroso, Freudians thought all persons were born asocial with aggressive and sexual id-wishes, and that, although many persons were socialized into social beings, the delinquents remained somewhat asocial because of faulty parent–child relationships. These persons tended to think of the delinquent as an abnormal person for whom his or her delinquency was an individual trait.[5]

On the other hand, sociologists thought that delinquency was a property of an underprivileged group, class, or sector of society. They claimed these groups acquired this property as a result of: *(1)* their delinquent subculture, *(2)* their disadvantaged, powerless, and deprived status, and *(3)* alienative and discriminative policies of groups in power. They asserted that societal pressures generated conditions of *anomie* and deregulation for these groups and parti-cularly for certain individuals in these groups. Other sociologists saw *conflict* as the cause of crime and delinquency. Their view was that conflict existed in class structure. To wit, the middle class dominated the lower class, and lower class boys, in turn, negated middle-class values, isolating themselves in a delinquent subcul-ture. They also viewed religious, political, and interest conflicts, as generative of crime and delinquency.[6]

Federal Involvement

Although delinquency control is largely a state or local matter in America, federal agencies have historically given advice and financial aid.

The first White House Conference on Children founded the Children's Bureau in the Department of Labor in 1912. The purpose of the Children's Bureau was to "have a central office where facts of child life could be collected, reviewed, and inter-preted to individuals and organized groups, thus making possible intelligent action and reducing needless experimentation." The bureau provided technical assistance, arranged research studies and distributed information to agencies dealing with juvenile delinquents.

The Juvenile Delinquency Prevention and Control Act of 1968 was, in part, a concerned nation's response to the continuing problem of juvenile delinquency. It was administered by the Office of Juvenile Delinquency and Youth, in the Social and Rehabilitative Service of the U.S. Department of Health, Education and Welfare. The Act was designed to help states, local communities, and public and private nonprofit agencies develop their capabilities in delinquency prevention and control programs. Assistance was made available through grants and technical assistance.

In 1972, a separation took place between the delinquency prevention programs outside the juvenile justice system and delinquency control activities within the juvenile justice system. The former were funded by the department of Health, Education, and Welfare (HEW) and the latter entrusted to the Law Enforcement Assistance Administration (LEAA). In 1974, the Juvenile Justice and Delinquency Prevention Act brought both the prevention and control functions within the jurisdiction of the U.S. Department of Justice, Law Enforcement Assistance Administration. To administer a unified national program, this Act also created the Office of Juvenile Justice and Delinquency Prevention. The emphasis of the 1974 Act was on diversion of juvenile offenders to community-based treatment, and deincarceration of offenders. The U.S. Supreme Court also came into the picture. After the juvenile court had enjoyed immunity from interference for over half a century, the Supreme Court cracked down on juvenile courts in the mid-1960s requiring them to safeguard children's rights.

HISTORICAL CONSEQUENCES FOR CHILDREN

A glance through history reveals that children have been treated in a variety of ways over the last 500 years in Europe and America. The early Americans brought with them the traumatic lessons of the breakdown of feudalism and benevolent notions of *Parens Patriae*. History had many more problems awaiting youth. Problems were created by immigration, culture changes, rapid industrialization, urbanization, wars, and breakdown of family systems. Children became victims of all of these changes. Some of the consequences of these historical changes are discussed below.

Deteriorating Family Government

The colonists stressed the need for disciplining children in the family. To them, disobedience to parents was both a sin and a crime. Children guilty of disrespect to parents were deemed deserving of severe punishment. According to Rothman, the colonists relied on the institutions of family, church, and a network of community relations as important weapons in the battle against sin and crime. The well-ordered family was considered a prelude to a well-ordered society; the town's good order rested upon family authority. Parents were asked to "govern their children well, restrain, reprove, and correct them. A Christian householder should *rule well his own house*."[7] Children were to be reared to be serviceable to the community. If parents neglected their duty, the community had the right to remove the child and place it in another household.

It should be remembered that the colonists viewed the family as a socializer and designed their almshouses in the 1700s to resemble the family dwelling.

Crumbling Social Order

America began to witness a great change in the early 1800s as a result of increasing immigration from outside and internal migration of population. Growing industry attracted many Americans to large cities in search of jobs. In large, impersonal cities, youth roamed about in the "streets of vice," visiting prostitutes, night clubs, and theaters. The Puritan critics thought that society was going to ruin itself without family and community discipline. This

perception of a growing lack of discipline in society brought about
the rise of a new kind of institution for children known as the
House of Refuge. The House of Refuge was an ancestor of the
present-day training school. Americans took comfort in the belief
that the House of Refuge would wean away unruly youth from the
corrupting influence of the taverns, gambling halls, and brothels.
Laws were passed to incarcerate youth in these institutions. Incarcerated youth were mostly children of immigrants and the poor
whom law makers sought to make compliant citizens in the interest
of social stability. Managers of the Houses of Refuge were very
optimistic that "the minds of young children, naturally pliant,
could, by early instruction, be formed and molded to society's
wishes."[8]

After their release from an institution, children were indentured to work in private homes for several years. They worked as
servants until such time that the master decided to release them.
Children were subjected to this treatment in the name of children's
protection, social order, community cohesion, and family stability.

Damaging Urban Life

As growing American cities attracted tens of thousands of
new families, many began to lose control of their children. Problems of adjustment were more acute in the case of those families
who moved from rural Europe or rural America. City life with all
of its pressures and pulls corrupted youth, particularly in crowded
slums, and weakened the family's hold on its children. A social
reformer wrote, "By some cruel alchemy, we take the sturdiest of
European peasantry and at once destroy in a large measure its
power to rear to decent livelihood the first generation of offsprings
upon our soil."[9] In order to beef up the weakening controls of the
family, school, and other authorities, reformers were instrumental
in getting several authority laws passed by legislatures. The belief
that city life corrupts morals was so pervasive that these reformers
arranged to locate children's institutions in rural areas.

Child-Saving Movement

According to Platt, "Contemporary programs of delinquency control can be traced to the enterprising reforms of the child savers who, at the end of the nineteenth century, helped to create special judicial and correctional institutions for the labeling, processing, and management of 'troublesome' youth."[10] They were the inventors of present-day delinquency laws. Who were the "child savers"? They were a group of middle-class reformers, altruists, and humanitarians who were dedicated to the cause of disadvantaged persons. Platt[11] makes a very strong argument that these child savers, though well-intentioned, overreacted in imposing middle-class morality on society through juvenile laws.

> . . . They brought attention to—and, in doing so, invented—new categories of youthful misbehavior which had been hitherto unappreciated. . . . Although the child savers were rhetorically concerned with protecting children from the physical and moral dangers of an increasingly industrialized and urban society, their remedies seemed to aggravate the problem.

The child-saving movement in Chicago was mobilized through the efforts of feminist reformers who were quite concerned about the adverse changes taking place in the traditional family system. The ladies leading this movement were Jane Addams, Louise Bowen, and Julia Lathrope. These leaders were quite influential both through their parents and husbands, and used their influence to instigate special laws for juveniles and create new institutions for their reformation.[12] Despite their good intentions, it is alleged that these feminist reformers imposed their Puritan middle-class family standards on lower-class children. They wanted to reestablish the authority of parents or parent-surrogates over children which the parents had lost during industrialization and urbanization.

> Their central interest was in the normative behavior of youth—their recreation, leisure, education, outlook on life, attitude to authority, family relationship, and personal morality. . . . They were most

active in extending governmental control over a whole range of youthful activities that had been previously ignored or dealt with informally. . . . The child savers were prohibitionists in a general sense who believed that social progress depended on efficient law enforcement, strict supervision of children's leisure and recreation, and the regulation of illicit pleasures.[13]

In their effort to restore and maintain proper order in the family, the reformers seemed to be on the parents' side rather than that of the children. Most of the laws regulated children's conduct, but parents' conduct was not questioned. Child savers did not make a distinction between delinquents and predelinquents. With their emphasis on prevention of delinquency, they regulated the activities of "predelinquents," considering that youth so labeled were likely to become delinquents. Child savers helped to bring in the juvenile court at the turn of the century. They also supported reform schools (or industrial schools) and probation. Thus, they extended governmental control over the "predelinquent."[14]

Platt also argues that corporate business had a vested interest in child labor laws and compulsory education laws (in removing children from small business and reeducating them for large-scale industrial production).[15] Without entering into this controversy of political or economic motives of big business, one theme emerges clearly from the 19th century penology. That theme is preoccupation with the unruly elements in society, and the taming of these persons into orderly individuals who would conform to middle-class values and needs. This taming and training took place either in youth institutions or in families. It was believed youth must develop habits of industry, proper skills, good manners, discipline, conformity, and law-abidingness. To this end, Houses of Refuge were built in the early 1800s, probation was begun in the middle 1800s, and the juvenile court was instituted toward the end of the century.

Parent–Child Relations

In formulating measures for control and prevention of delinquency, the tenure of parent–child relations looms very large in importance. Parents have their own problems which color their relationship with children. They tend to hold their children responsible for their troubles and anxieties. Lloyd deMause thinks that parent–child relations have passed through several modes during the course of history. There were times when infants were killed (antiquity to the 4th century), were abandoned to wet nurses, monasteries, or foster families (4th to 14th centuries), were molded to suit their parents' wishes (14th to 17th centuries), were conquered by intrusive parents attacking their mind with threats and guilt (18th century), and were socialized to conform (19th to mid-20th centuries).[16]

> . . . the raising of a child became less a process of conquering its will than of training it, guiding it into proper paths, teaching it to conform, socializing it. The socializing mode is still thought of by most people as the only model within which discussion of child care can proceed, and it has been the source of all twentieth-century psychological models, from Freud's "channeling of impulses" to Skinner's behaviorism.[17]

The socializing process can easily be coercive and, at times, violent. To Steinmetz and Straus, violence seems as typical of family relationships as love. Starting with slaps and going on to torture and murder, the family provides a prime setting for every degree of physical violence.[18] Gil believes physical abuse of children is more often an indication of a prevailing pattern of caretaker–child interaction in a given home than an isolated incident.[19] There is ample evidence of this in case records of juvenile courts. Many runaways have sad stories to tell of physical and sexual abuse in their homes. Similarly, children also threaten their parents with physical violence and generate all kinds of problems for their parents. In the nuclear family, there are few mediators to intervene between parents and children. Many parents who have failed with their children come to the courts in sheer desperation. Unfortunately, some of these parents use the court as a dumping ground for their children. Such parents simply neglect their children. To protect children and parents from each other, and also to protect the interests of society, industrial societies developed a variety of laws and juvenile justice agencies (police, courts, correctional institutions). Although judicial intervention is necessary in some cases, its excessive use can be more harmful than helpful. Overreliance on law and a frequent resort to formalized legislative solutions to youth and family problems is a typical reaction in complex industrial societies. This reaction constitutes a process of overcriminalization.

JUVENILE JUSTICE: A CASE OF OVERCRIMINALIZATION, OVERPROCESSING, OVERINCARCERATION, DENIAL OF DUE PROCESS PROTECTIONS, AND LACK OF DEMAND FOR ACCOUNTABILITY

Overcriminalization

Criminalization is a process by which a powerful group in society creates a law and applies that law against persons or groups whom they want to control. Hartjen states that persons may seek to criminalize a behavior when they experience a threat to their interests. Whether persons are successful in criminalizing the behavior of others is contingent upon the relative power of persons experiencing the threat and the persons assumed to be its source.[20]

Criminalization is most likely to be directed toward the behavior of the poor and powerless. Children and youth have been particularly susceptible to the criminalization process. To illustrate, laws which gave birth to the juvenile court in 1899 resulted in the criminalization of much juvenile behavior that was theretofore noncriminal. Today, state statutes allow the juvenile court to exercise jurisdiction over both youth who have committed acts which would be considered crimes if they were adults and youth who run away from home, are truant from school, violate curfew restrictions, or are labeled as "incorrigible," "wayward" or "beyond control." The court also has jurisdiction over youth who are in an environment injurious to their welfare, or who do not receive proper care, supervision, or discipline from their parents, custodian, or guardian, or whose parents, custodians, or guardian are unable to discharge their responsibilities to and for the child, or who are in need of special care or treatment, or who are destitute, homeless, abandoned, or in a condition of neglect. It is evident that the state, through the juvenile court, has authority to intervene in the lives of youth and families for almost any reason it desires. This enormous, frequently unrestrained, power possessed by the juvenile court is a direct result of overcriminalization of the behavior of children and youth.

Research studies indicate that juvenile court jurisdiction over youth behavior which does not present a danger to other persons or property (status offenses) does not serve the interest of youths, the juvenile justice system, or taxpayers. Decriminalization of status offenses will be considered in a subsequent chapter.

Overprocessing

The number of youth processed by the juvenile justice system is staggering (see Figure 1.1). Each year, approximately 8% of youth within the jurisdiction of the juvenile court are arrested. About 4% of these youths are referred to the juvenile court, with 2% of these having a court hearing.

Research studies show that, whether caught by the police or undetected, about 80% of all juveniles commit one or two offenses and stop. To wit, most youth become delinquent, but grow out of it. A few youths become chronic offenders.[21] The massive cohort study by Figlio et al. demonstrated that the juvenile justice system does a commendable job of isolating these chronic offenders.[22]

There is convincing evidence that overprocessing of youth has a deleterious impact on youths and reduces the amount of time the juvenile justice system has to deal with youth who present a serious threat to other persons or property. Diversion, a response to overprocessing which has taken many forms, will be examined in a later chapter.

Figure 1.1. The Juvenile Justice Mill: The Number of Juveniles Processed by Juvenile Justice Agencies

Arrested	2,540,348[a]
Processed by juvenile court	1,252,700[b]
Detained in jails, detention centers	1,000,000[c]
Institutionalized	85,109[d]

[a]Prorated for population of 200 millions. FBI reported 2,078,459 for an estimated population of 179,191,000 in the year 1975. (PINS and children beyond control not included.)

[b]Estimated number of delinquency cases. Source: U. S. Department of Justice, Juvenile Court Statistics, Washington, 1974.

[c-d]Sarri, Rosemary C., Under Lock and Key, Juveniles in Jails and Detention. Ann Arbor, Mich.: National Assessment of Juvenile Corrections, University of Michigan, 1974, p. 64.

Overincarceration

Each year, approximately 1,000,000 youths are held in jails and juvenile detention centers, and about 85,000 youths are committed to public training schools, halfway houses, camps, and group homes. Although some states, to the chagrin of many juvenile court judges, have enacted laws which prohibit the incarceration of status offenders in state training schools, a number of states continue to dump these youths into institutions. Furthermore, most states have maintained their policy of permitting juvenile court personnel to hold status offenders in jails and detention centers.

Although there is growing evidence that incarceration of youths in institutions has adverse consequences for youth, efforts of youth advocates and the federal government to deinstitutionalize youths who have been incarcerated for committing an act that would not have been a crime if committed by an adult have met with limited success. One reason for the failure to deinstitutionalize noncriminal children is that many juvenile court judges, state bureaucrats, and those who have a financial interest in maintaining expensive, ineffective, and inhumane institutions, continue to present substantial obstacles to full-scale deinstitutionalization in most states.

In a subsequent chapter, deinstitutionalization efforts by states will be examined and recommendations regarding the implementation of more efficacious deinstitutionalization policies, practices, and programs will be presented.

Denial of Due Process Protections

In recent years, the U.S. Supreme Court has held that juveniles have a constitutional right to certain due process protections. The National Assessment of Juvenile Corrections, University of Michigan (NAJC) found that the average juvenile court only complies with about 70% of Supreme Court mandates requiring the provision of due process protections for juveniles.[23] Specifically, the NAJC determined that there was not *full* compliance by juvenile courts with the following Supreme Court mandates: *(1)* use of a standard of proof beyond a reasonable doubt during the adjudication stage of a delinquency proceeding in which a juvenile may be committed to a state institution, *(2)* provision of a written notice of charges to youth, *(3)* appointment of counsel at adjudication and waiver hearings, and *(4)* the right to cross-examine witnesses.

A comprehensive treatment of due process compliance in the

juvenile court, including a list of indicators which can be utilized to measure due process compliance in a juvenile court, is presented in a later chapter.

Lack of Demand for Accountability

The lack of accountability in juvenile justice is evidenced by the paucity of reviews of activities of juvenile courts by State Supreme Courts, the dearth of monitoring of court services by state agencies, the marginal role of the prosecutor and defense attorney in the juvenile court, the lack of valid and reliable information about youth processed by the court, and the limited influence which external organizations have on the court.

If delinquency prevention and control agencies are to be held accountable, residents of a locality served by a juvenile court must be organized so as to possess the power, authority, and expertise necessary to expeditiously eliminate, modify, merge, expand, create, monitor, evaluate, and investigate the policies, practices, and programs of said agencies when the need arises. A subsequent chapter in this book provides a detailed explanation as to how this capacity can be developed through the use of "power advocacy" in juvenile justice.

OUTLINE FOR CHAPTER 2

Problems in Juvenile Justice

Introduction
Juvenile Arrests: A Problem of Police Discretion
    Volume of Arrests
    Police Response
    Factors Affecting Police Decisions at Encounters
    Police Discretion: The Need for Guidelines
    Station Adjustment: More Choices, More Discretion
Juvenile Court: The Unfulfilled Promise
    Parens Patriae Doctrine
Failings of the Juvenile Court
    Problems Too Deep
    Probation Inadequate
    Recidivism Rate Remained High
    Delinquency Rate Growing
    The Court's Vulnerability: Externally
      Too Many Masters to Serve
      Inferior Status of the Court
      Too Many Demands
      Court's Dependence on Outside Agencies
    The Court's Vulnerability: Internally
      Chronic State of Overload
      Faulty Recording System
      The Stigma
      Hurried Trials
      Informal Hearing and Denial of Due Process
      Kent vs. United States
        Brief Facts
        Grounds for the Petition

Chapter 2

PROBLEMS IN JUVENILE JUSTICE

INTRODUCTION

Many problems of delinquent youths are caused by an inappropriate reaction on the part of the juvenile justice system. Whether or not a youth is arrested and processed further depends largely on the discretion of a police officer. How wisely a police officer uses his or her discretion depends on several factors: the police department's policy, the police officer's personal background, attitude of the youth, education, inservice training, youth demeanor, and police–youth relationships in the community. Police are the chief diverters of youths. Although they divert about one-half of all youths with whom they have contact, they could divert more youths without increasing any hazard to the community.

The juvenile court has failed to have a positive impact on youths. The problem of delinquency is too deeply rooted in society to be alleviated effectively during a short court session. Juvenile courts are beset with such problems as: *(1)* inferior status, *(2)* chronic state of overload, *(3)* hurried trials, *(4)* faulty recording practices, and *(5)* limited funding.

Overincarceration of youths in jails, detention centers, and correctional institutions continues to be a major problem in juvenile justice. The problems of the police, juvenile courts, and juvenile institutions will now be examined in greater detail.

JUVENILE ARRESTS: A PROBLEM OF POLICE DISCRETION

Volume of Arrests

Juvenile arrests from 1973 to 1976 have fluctuated from a low of 1,683,073 in 1974 to a high of 2,078,459 in 1975. FBI figures depend on the number of agencies reporting their crime figures. In 1975, figures were reported for an estimated population of 179,191,000 (which was not the total population of the United States), and the number of arrests for persons under age 18 exceeded two million (see Table 2.1). If figures were available for the entire population, the number of juvenile arrests would far exceed two million. These FBI figures do not include the arrests of many status offenders.

Police Response

Because of the large volume of arrests every year, it is imperative that police officers respond appropriately to juvenile misconduct. An overly harsh reaction is likely to antagonize youth against the police and create a negative police–youth relationship. Usually a youth's encounter with police constitutes his initial contact with the juvenile justice system. The manner in which the police officer handles this encounter has far-reaching consequences for the youth. To quote the President's Commission on Law Enforcement and Administration of Justice:[1]

Table 2.1. Total Arrests by Age in the United States, 1973-76

Offense charged	1973 Grand total all ages	1973 Ages under 15	1973 Ages under 18	1973 Ages 18 and over	1974 Grand total all ages	1974 Ages under 15	1974 Ages under 18	1974 Ages 18 and over
TOTAL	6,499,864	614,716	1,717,366	4,782,498	6,179,406	606,548	1,683,073	4,496,333
Percent distribution [1]	100.0	9.5	26.4	73.6	100.0	9.8	27.2	72.8
Criminal homicide:								
(a) Murder and nonnegligent manslaughter	14,399	246	1,497	12,902	13,818	206	1,399	12,419
(b) Manslaughter by negligence	2,996	83	363	2,633	2,226	40	223	2,003
Forcible rape	19,198	813	3,772	15,426	17,804	771	3,455	14,349
Robbery	101,894	11,015	34,374	67,520	108,481	9,984	35,345	73,136
Aggravated assault	154,891	8,200	26,270	128,621	154,514	7,943	26,300	128,214
Burglary—breaking or entering	316,272	73,139	170,228	146,044	340,697	73,957	181,689	159,008
Larceny—theft	644,190	146,910	310,452	333,738	729,661	165,214	356,695	372,966
Auto theft	118,380	17,736	66,868	51,512	107,226	15,699	59,183	48,043
Violent crime [2]	290,382	20,244	65,913	224,469	294,617	18,904	66,499	228,118
Percent distribution [1]	100.0	7.0	22.7	77.3	100.0	6.4	22.6	77.4
Property crime [3]	1,078,842	237,785	547,548	531,294	1,177,584	254,870	597,567	580,017
Percent distribution [1]	100.0	22.0	50.8	49.2	100.0	21.6	50.7	49.3
Other assaults	275,105	21,013	53,044	222,061	269,643	21,761	54,205	215,438
Arson	11,096	4,420	6,491	4,605	10,756	4,098	6,318	4,438
Forgery and counterfeiting	41,975	729	4,687	37,318	39,741	934	5,268	34,473
Fraud	85,467	686	3,159	82,308	91,176	1,361	4,764	86,412
Embezzlement	5,612	87	429	5,183	5,891	84	454	5,437
Stolen property; buying, receiving, possessing	70,238	7,121	23,738	46,500	76,943	7,923	26,406	50,537
Vandalism	121,011	51,377	83,428	37,583	146,261	61,621	100,492	45,769
Weapons; carrying, possessing, etc.	115,918	4,756	18,635	97,283	119,189	4,643	19,000	100,189
Prostitution and commercialized vice	45,308	150	1,769	43,539	53,309	173	2,130	51,179
Sex offenses (except forcible rape and prostitution)	48,673	3,698	9,784	38,889	44,375	3,480	9,953	34,422
Narcotic drug laws	484,242	16,222	127,316	356,926	454,948	15,035	118,460	336,488
Gambling	54,938	270	1,544	53,394	45,900	290	1,896	44,004
Offenses against family and children	42,784	222	994	41,790	34,902	1,626	3,707	31,195
Driving under the influence	653,914	242	9,026	644,888	616,549	254	8,818	607,731
Liquor laws	183,813	7,178	74,690	109,123	191,213	7,581	79,323	111,890
Drunkenness	1,189,489	4,207	34,722	1,154,767	911,837	3,258	28,638	883,199
Disorderly conduct	461,553	36,114	103,556	357,997	544,321	36,844	109,440	434,881
Vagrancy	50,310	1,272	6,016	44,294	32,802	1,070	4,619	28,183
All other offenses (except traffic)	848,835	87,475	231,018	617,817	757,040	75,998	199,401	557,639
Suspicion	40,927	4,383	13,090	27,837	33,363	3,362	10,672	22,691
Curfew and loitering law violations	118,003	33,651	118,003		70,167	17,174	70,167	
Runaways	178,433	71,331	178,433		154,653	64,164	154,653	

Source: FBI: *Crime in the United States, 1973-1976.*
Washington, D. C., U. S. Government Printing Office.

Whether or not a juvenile becomes involved in the juvenile justice system usually depends upon the outcome of an encounter with the police. Such encounters are frequent, especially in the crowded inner city.

Some of them grow out of a criminal act of significant proportions: The juveniles have been caught in the act, or are being sought,

Table 2.1.   (Continued)

Offense charged	1975				1976			
	Grand total all ages	Ages under 15	Ages under 18	Ages 18 and over	Grand total all ages	Ages under 15	Ages under 18	Ages 18 and over
TOTAL	8,013,645	716,206	2,078,459	5,935,186	7,912,348	665,781	1,973,254	5,939,094
Percent distribution [1]	100.0	8.9	25.9	74.1	100.0	8.4	24.9	75.1
Criminal homicide:								
(a) Murder and nonnegligent manslaughter	16,485	184	1,573	14,912	14,113	190	1,302	12,811
(b) Manslaughter by negligence	3,041	80	368	2,673	2,650	43	275	2,375
Forcible rape	21,963	867	3,863	18,100	21,687	915	3,745	17,942
Robbery	129,788	12,515	44,470	85,318	110,296	10,156	36,990	73,306
Aggravated assault	202,217	10,600	35,512	166,705	192,753	9,552	32,678	160,075
Burglary—breaking or entering	449,155	90,189	236,192	212,963	406,821	78,275	209,396	197,425
Larceny—theft	958,938	192,495	432,019	526,919	928,078	173,535	399,235	528,843
Motor vehicle theft	120,224	17,290	65,564	54,660	110,708	14,726	58,279	52,429
Violent crime [3]	370,453	24,166	85,418	285,035	338,849	20,813	74,715	264,134
Percent distribution [1]	100.0	6.5	23.1	76.9	100.0	6.1	22.0	78.0
Property crime [3]	1,528,317	299,974	733,775	794,542	1,445,607	266,536	666,910	778,697
Percent distribution [1]	100.0	19.6	48.0	52.0	100.0	18.4	46.1	53.9
Other assaults	352,648	26,280	69,965	282,683	354,010	25,907	69,904	294,106
Arson	14,589	4,904	7,727	6,862	14,534	4,626	7,601	6,933
Forgery and counterfeiting	57,803	1,215	7,320	50,483	55,791	1,090	6,681	49,110
Fraud	146,253	851	4,665	141,588	161,429	879	4,614	156,815
Embezzlement	9,302	157	679	8,623	8,218	103	525	7,693
Stolen property; buying, receiving, possessing	100,903	9,445	32,891	68,012	92,055	8,142	28,940	63,115
Vandalism	175,865	66,663	115,046	60,819	175,082	60,569	109,712	65,370
Weapons; carrying, possessing, etc	130,933	5,127	21,365	109,568	121,722	4,549	19,649	102,073
Prostitution and commercialized vice	50,229	177	2,362	47,867	58,648	205	2,570	56,078
Sex offenses (except forcible rape and prostitution)	50,837	3,928	10,876	39,961	51,776	3,779	9,902	41,874
Narcotic drug laws	508,189	16,225	122,857	385,332	500,540	15,514	119,522	381,018
Gambling	49,469	263	1,763	47,706	65,437	392	2,547	62,890
Offenses against family and children	53,332	2,884	6,271	47,061	58,249	1,595	4,198	54,051
Driving under the influence	908,680	289	17,020	891,660	837,910	254	17,264	820,646
Liquor laws	267,057	9,429	105,813	161,244	302,943	',679	108,934	194,009
Drunkenness	1,176,121	4,243	41,457	1,134,664	1,071,131	..866	39,750	1,031,381
Disorderly conduct	632,561	34,989	120,278	512,283	545,639	35,845	113,898	431,741
Vagrancy	59,277	1,296	5,323	53,954	32,731	1,741	5,848	26,883
All other offenses (except traffic)	1,037,754	95,020	256,568	781,186	1,330,969	107,901	295,952	1,035,017
Suspicion	29,098	2,365	7,718	21,380	31,298	2,363	8,213	23,085
Curfew and loitering law violations	112,117	29,974	112,117	....	88,601	24,217	88,601	....
Runaways	188,817	76,258	188,817	....	166,529	65,173	166,529	....

or there is reason to believe that they answer the description given by a complainant. In such instances, the contact is very likely to lead to further processing by the juvenile justice system.

On the other hand, many encounters are based on a relatively minor violation, or not on a specific crime at all but on the policeman's sense that something is wrong. He may suspect that a crime has happened or is about to happen. Or he may believe the juvenile's conduct is offensive, insolent, or in some way improper. On such occasions, the policeman has a relatively great range of choices: He can pass by. He can stop for a few words of general banter. He can ask the juveniles their names, where they live, where they are going. He can question them about what has been happening in the neighborhood. He can search them, order them to disperse or move on, or check with the station for records and recent neighborhood offenses. He can send or take them home, where he may warn their parents to keep them off the street. Suspicion, even perhaps without very specific grounds for it, may on occasion lead him to bring them in to the station for further questioning or checking.

In any given encounter, the policeman's selection among alternatives may vary considerably among departments and among individual officers. It is governed to some extent by departmental practice, either explicitly enunciated or tacitly understood. Such policies are difficult to evolve—indeed, in many instances they could not be specific enough to be helpful without being too rigid to accommodate the vast variety of street situations. Nevertheless, it is important that, wherever possible, police forces formulate guidelines for policemen in their dealings with juveniles.

Factors Affecting Police Decisions at Encounters

Whether a police officer decides to make an arrest depends on several factors. One important factor affecting the decision of the officer is the policy and practice of his or her department. Police departments differ greatly in their orientation. Another factor is the police officer's attitude which is a product of his or her background, education, and past experiences with youth and the community in which he is working.

A study of juvenile–police encounters revealed that 72% resulted from citizens' complaints. Consequently, the police officer must pacify the complainant, satisfy the requirements of the department, justify it to the community, and yet be fair to the youth. The officer, often without specialized training in dealing with youth, must satisfy all of these parties and make a decision on the scene under the pressure of the moment.

Police Discretion: The Need for Guidelines

Certainly discretion is an essential component of police decisions. The important thing is that it be used fairly, uniformly, and in the best interest of youth and victims of youth crime. Furthermore, the discretion used should also not evoke the criticism of superiors in the police department, prosecutors, and the courts. Police discretion in dealing with juveniles is a grave responsibility for officers, and the public should help them in using their discretion properly. Kobetz and Bosarge suggest that legislative and administrative guidelines should be set up for the guidance of police officers.[2] The 1973 Conference of International Association of Chiefs of Police (IACP) made the following recommendations:[3]

1. It is recommended that all law enforcement agencies revise rules and regulations manuals to include policy guidelines on the use of discretionary judgment and include examples of situations where discretionary judgment to arrest may be utilized by police officers.
2. It is recommended that all law enforcement agencies conduct training programs both at the recruit and in-service levels to affirm the department's position on the use of discretionary judgment and to acquaint officers with situations in which discretion may be exercised.
3. It is recommended that all law enforcement agencies establish internal procedures to review the exercise of discretionary decision-making and take appropriate disciplinary action when discretion is misused or subverted to a wrong purpose.

Station Adjustment: More Choices, More Discretion

At station adjustment, the juvenile may be dealt with either by a juvenile officer or by a specialized juvenile unit. Several commissions and the IACP Conference participants have recommended that all police departments in medium to larger cities establish a specialized juvenile unit which should keep working 24 hours every day to meet the emergency needs of the youth.[4] The staff of these units should be well trained in handling youth problems. They screen every case thoroughly to see if it can be disposed of through informal and discretionary pre-judicial procedures without resort to the juvenile courts. The President's Crime Commission (1967) has expressed its firm belief in discretionary dispositions in the following words:[5]

> Informal and discretionary pre-judicial dispositions already are a formally recognized part of the process to a far greater extent in the juvenile than in the criminal justice system. The primacy of the rehabilitative goal in dealing with juveniles, the limited effectiveness of the formal processes of the juvenile justice system, the labeling inherent in adjudicating children delinquents, the inability of the formal system to reach the influences—family, school, labor market, recreational opportunities—that shape the life of a youngster, the limited disposition options available to the juvenile judge, the limitations of personnel and diagnostic and treatment facilities, the lack of community support—all of these factors give *pre-judicial dispositions an especially important role with respect to juveniles.*
>
> Yet on balance, it is clear to the Commission that informal pre-judicial handling is preferable to formal treatment in many cases and should be used more broadly. The possibilities for rehabilitation appear to be optimal where community-based resources are used on a basis as nearly consensual as possible.

Since more choices are available to the juvenile officers or specialized juvenile unit, they can use more discretion. Some of the dispositional alternatives which may be available to them are as follows:[6]

1. Release.
2. Release to parents (warning and release).
3. Referral to social agencies.
4. Referral to the juvenile court without detention.
5. Referral to the juvenile court with detention.

Which of the several alternatives is most suitable in a certain case? It is never an easy decision. Among other things, the hearing officers in a specialized juvenile unit should consider the following:[7]

1. The age of the child.
2. The nature and severity of the offense.
3. The juvenile's prior contact with the police.
4. The juvenile's attitude toward accepting and cooperating with the efforts to help rehabilitate him.
5. The juvenile's need for professional assistance as determined by his physical and mental characteristics.
6. The ability of the child's parents to acknowledge their awareness of the seriousness of their child's involvement with the police and to control and discipline their child.
7. The rights of the complainant—injustice is not done to the victim/complainant through over-emphasis on the juvenile offender; and the social tranquility of the community is not sacrificed because police fail to deal with delinquents in a positive manner.

It is generally agreed that the police should accept some limitations on their discretion. They should not have discretionary authority to make detention decisions as this responsibility should rest with the court. If a juvenile is taken into police custody, the juvenile's rights and those of his or her parents must be observed.

Informal adjustment of juvenile cases by police officers varies from jurisdiction to jurisdiction. The Kansas City Police Department settles less than 10% of its juvenile cases informally, whereas the Des Moines, Iowa, Police Department settles 50 to 60% of its juvenile cases.[8]

JUVENILE COURT: THE UNFULFILLED PROMISE

Of all the components of the juvenile justice system, the juvenile court seems to have been the main target of adverse criticism. This is understandable in view of the fact that the juvenile court sits at the heart of the system. The juvenile court was founded in 1899 to protect the child from his or her condition of parental neglect or dependency, and to take necessary action if the child was found committing a status offense or delinquent act. Expectancies from the court were so many and so onerous that the court could not fulfill its promises.

Parens Patriae *Doctrine*

This doctrine was transplanted from England with some modifications. The doctrine of *parens patriae* originally was used to explain the source of the crown's power to maintain the feudalistic structure which required the orderly transfer of feudal duties from one generation to the next. Its extension in the past had been limited to intrafamily, aristocratic custody fights.[9] Later on, chancery courts were created by the king as *parens patriae* (father of his country) to protect children in need of protection. In the United States, the State established its guardianship over unprotected children through the juvenile court.[10]

> The idea of separating children from their parents actually developed from the English poor laws, which not only treated poverty as something "bad" and in need of isolation, but also permitted the apprenticeship of the children of poor persons to merchants and craftsmen. In the United States, this concept was adopted and expanded to cover the unchristian and uneducated child as well as the poor child. The doctrine of *parens patriae* became the pet phrase employed to legitimate separation of child and parent and to regulate children by the state for economic and class reasons.

The chancery court, however, dealt only with neglected and dependent children, not with children accused of criminal law violations. The American reformers wanted to diagnose and treat delinquent youth in a special way which was not possible in adult courts. All this culminated in the creation of the first juvenile court in Chicago in 1899.

Different people had different expectations from the juvenile court. The charity workers (or social workers) expected the juvenile court to focus on the individual for his personal reformation, and the settlement house workers saw social conditions as the target for change.[11] Settlement house workers favored a group-work approach. Treatment was to be focused on the child's home and family. The probation officer was supposed to be a central figure on the court staff, combining in himself or herself the dual role of a supervisor and a counselor for the youth. He was also supposed to work with the family and the community for the best interest of the youth.

FAILINGS OF THE JUVENILE COURT

Problems Too Deep

Problems generated by urbanization were too deep to be dealt with effectively by the court. Forces unleashed by immigration, internal migration, and rapid industrialization and urbanization created such a state of norm erosion that the court had little impact. The court could at best deal with the child and his or her family, and then only if the family cooperated and had some strengths left in it. If the family were completely depleted in its strength, only a big effort at the community level could be of some help. The court was limited in what it could do.

Probation Inadequate

The intention of the juvenile court was to deal with youth in the community under probation supervision, but probation remained inadequate to the task. There was increasing resort to the incarceration of children in institutions. One-third of all juveniles charged with delinquency were sent to state reformatories or transferred to the criminal courts. Almost two-thirds of "delinquent" girls were committed to state and local institutions.[12] This problem of unnecessary incarceration has persisted over the decades.

The probation officer, who was supposed to be a family tutor on techniques of child care and household management, could find very little time for family counseling. He was too busy with the court and his office. He was supposed to be a mentor and a guide to his client, but he had too many youths in his case load for such individual care. He was supposed to be a procurer of community services for the probationers, but a probation officer was only rarely equipped as an effective community worker. Although he remained unable to render all these social services to his clients, he found himself more and more drawn into the role of supervising them as expected by his agency or the courts. He was increasingly pressured to expand his role as a law enforcement agent even at the cost of abandoning his counseling role.

Recidivism Rate Remained High

In an outstanding follow-up study conducted by Healy and Bronner, the recidivism rate for youth handled by the Chicago Juvenile Court showed up as fairly high. Published about a quarter of a century after the inception of the Chicago Juvenile Court, this study can be regarded as representative of the Court's functioning.[13]

> Tracing the lives of several hundred youthful repeated offenders studied long ago by us and treated by ordinary so-called correctional methods reveals much repetition of offense. This is represented by the astonishing figures of 61% failure for males . . . and 46% failure for girls. . . . Thus in over one-half of the cases in this particular series, juvenile delinquency has continued into careers of vice and crime.

It was soon realized that the juvenile court was not a panacea for the problems of the adolescent. Where Healy's study showed a high rate of failure, later on (in 1942), Shaw and McKay's study showed that boys who had one or more delinquent brothers showed a still higher recidivism rate of 72%.[14]

Delinquency Rate Growing

Delinquency is growing both in number and rate every year, as Table 2.2 shows. All courts—urban, semi-urban, and rural—are experiencing increased cases. The number of girls' delinquency cases disposed of by juvenile courts has been rising more rapidly than those of boys every year since 1965. Between 1964

Table 2.2. Estimated Number and Rate of Delinquency Cases Disposed of by Juvenile Courts in the United States, 1957-1974

Year	Estimated Delinquency Cases	Child Population 10-17 yrs of age (in thousands)	Rate[a]
1957	440,000	22,173	19.8
1958	470,000	23,443	20.0
1959	483,000	24,607	19.6
1960	510,000	25,368	20.1
1961	503,000	26,056	19.3
1962	555,000	26,989	20.6
1963	601,000	28,056	21.4
1964	686,000	29,244	23.5
1965	697,000	29,536	23.6
1966	745,000	30,124	24.7
1967	811,000	30,837	26.3
1968	900,000	31,566	28.5
1969	988,500	32,157	30.7
1970	1,052,000	32,614	32.3
1971	1,125,000	32,969	34.1
1972	1,112,500	33,120	33.6
1973	1,143,700	33,377	34.2
1974	1,252,700	33,365	37.5

[a]Based on the number of delinquency cases per 1000 U.S. child population 10-17 yrs of age.
   Source: U.S. Dept. of Justice, Juvenile Court Statistics, National Institute for Juvenile Justice and Delinquency Prevention, Washington, D.C., 1974, p. 15.

and 1974, girls' cases increased by 129%, and boys' cases by 67%.[15]

The Court's Vulnerability: Externally

In a consultant's paper written for the Task Force on Juvenile Delinquency and Youth Crime,[16] Vinter perceives the juvenile court as the most vulnerable institution in the judicial system. Several forces and conditions affect the court's ability to achieve its potential. First, let us look at some of the external forces hampering the court in its functions.

TOO MANY MASTERS TO SERVE.   The juvenile court has complex relationships with other organizations at both the local and state levels. The juvenile court's basic mandates are defined by the legislature, its proceedings can be reviewed and supervised by higher courts, and its operations are partially subject to fiscal and administrative decisions of various agencies, such as state welfare departments. . . . Much of its financial support is provided or curtailed by local government and the judge usually occupies his position by consent of the local electorate. . . . Both law and voter must be served by court performance.[17]

INFERIOR STATUS OF THE COURT.   The juvenile court does not enjoy a superior status in the hierarchy of courts. It is neither regarded well by lawyers nor respected highly by the welfare professions. The court's low salaries and low esteem attract very few qualified personnel. It can generally be said that ambitious persons in the legal profession do not aspire to judgeships in the juvenile courts.

TOO MANY DEMANDS.   The juvenile court has to adjudicate according to juvenile statutes, yet ensure that none of the legal rights of the children are violated. The police, schools, and other agencies in the community expect a judge to mete out exemplary punishments to delinquents and uphold public order. Yet the judge is also supposed to protect children and act in their best interest. "The court is expected simultaneously to preserve the institution of law, to enhance the legitimate interests of its clients, especially those of children, and to serve the welfare of the community while protecting public order."[18]

COURT'S DEPENDENCE ON OUTSIDE AGENCIES.   For case referrals, the juvenile court must depend upon several social agencies, such as welfare departments, children's aid clinics, the YMCA, group homes, schools, and churches. This referral process involves the court in several reciprocal obligations. The referring agency may expect the juvenile court to consider its wishes in deciding the case.

The Court's Vulnerability: Internally

The juvenile court attempts to be both a judicial and a service organization. This duality of roles is partially responsible for some of its internal problems.

CHRONIC STATE OF OVERLOAD.   There is an imbalance between the court's resources and the volume of cases it has to handle. Intake departments try to deflect and divert many cases to reduce the court's case load. Youths processed by the court present a wide range of problems, but the court does not have dispositional options available to deal with these problems.

FAULTY RECORDING SYSTEM.   According to Vinter, "systems for the recording, retention, retrieval, and usage of information are antiquated and less than reliable, usually depending only on manual techniques. . . . Much information is retained only in heads of workers and is never reported, whereas important decisions are sometimes unrecorded."[19] Computerized court-processing technology is required to eliminate this deficiency.

THE STIGMA.   The stigma of court disposition is real, no matter how the court attempts to hide it. In smaller communities, as one judge observed, "Everyone knows about juvenile court cases anyway." Lemert says:

> Such stigma, represented in modern society by a "record," gets translated into effective handicaps by heightened police surveillance, neighborhood isolation, lowered receptivity and tolerance by school officials, and rejection of youth by prospective employers.[20]

The Armed Forces are definitely allergic to delinquency records, and so are many other employers. These records are not easily expunged.

HURRIED TRIALS.   Murphy, who was the chief attorney with the Juvenile Office of the Legal Aid Society in Chicago, tells us how juveniles were made to admit their "offenses" in 2- to 5-minute conversations between a college student employed by the public defender's office and the parents of the child. The juvenile defendant had little to say.

> Since there are so many cases to be heard, the nine judges hearing them are under great pressure either to hasten trials into summary, ten-minute affairs or to talk the attorney representing the children into pleading them guilty in exchange for probation. . . . On a hot uncomfortable day, or on a day when the judges are in a hurry to get away to the golf links or the political clubhouse, it can be hard indeed to receive a fair, unhurried trial.[21]

If this is the situation in Chicago, it is no better in Los Angeles, where the average time given to a juvenile case was reported to be three minutes.[22]

INFORMAL HEARING AND DENIAL OF DUE PROCESS.   The original Juvenile Court Act (1899) passed by the Illinois legislature and the amendments to it that shortly followed brought together under one jurisdiction cases of dependency, neglect, and delinquency—the latter comprehending incorrigibles and children threatened by immoral associations as well as criminal law breakers. Hearings were to be informal and nonpublic, records confidential, children detained apart from adults, and a probation staff appointed. In short, children were not to be treated as criminals nor dealt with by the processes used for criminals.[23] The court had very wide jurisdiction over children. Since the juvenile court was a protector of children under the *parens patriae* doctrine, the court could proceed against anyone who was ungovernable or habitually disobedient or truant; who begged; who was habitually obscene or used profane language; or who so deported himself as wilfully to injure or endanger the morals or health of himself or others. As observed earlier in Chapter 1, the court could also assume jurisdiction over juveniles in whose case the care exercised by parent, guardian or custodian fell short of a legal standard for proper care. The court still holds this jurisdiction at the present time.

The court hearing is private and the proceedings resemble a conference called to bring forth facts rather than adversary proceedings. Juries are not used. Acting in the best interest of the child, the court tries to rehabilitate rather than punish the youth. With the wide powers enjoyed under the *parens patriae* doctrine, courts often disregarded the rights of children. Then came the historic decisions of the Supreme Court in the mid-1960s which greatly affected the informal nature of juvenile court proceedings. Although the full implications of these decisions will be dealt with in a subsequent chapter, here it will suffice to point out some of the glaring deficiencies in the juvenile court's procedure as highlighted by the U.S. Supreme Court.

KENT VS. UNITED STATES[24]

Brief Facts.   Kent, the petitioner, was arrested at the age of 16 in connection with charges of housebreaking, robbery, and rape. As a juvenile, he was subject to the exclusive jurisdiction of the District of Columbia Juvenile Court. However, that court could, after "full investigation," waive jurisdiction and remit him for trial to the U.S. District Court for the District of Columbia. The Juvenile Court did waive its jurisdiction over Kent and handed him over to the U.S. District Court for trial as an adult. The petitioner's counsel then filed a motion in the Juvenile Court. The motion requested:

  1.   A hearing on the question of waiver, and

2. Access to the Juvenile Court's social service file, which had been accumulated on petitioner during his probation for a prior offense.

The social service file was an important document, as it was going to be used in consideration of the waiver. The Juvenile Court judge did not rule on these motions. He held no hearing. He did not confer with petitioner or petitioner's parents or petitioner's counsel. He did not recite any reason for the waiver. The juvenile court entered an order waiving jurisdiction noting that this was done after the required "full investigation." Kent was tried by the District Court and convicted as an adult on six counts of robbery and housebreaking. He was acquitted on two rape counts by reasons of insanity. He was sentenced to serve 5 to 15 years on each of the six counts, with a total sentence of 30 to 90 years in prison.

Grounds for the Petition.   The petitioner pleaded that the Juvenile Court procedure leading to the waiver and the waiver order itself were invalid. The petitioner's counsel argued that petitioner's detention and interrogation were unlawful. He contended that the police failed to follow the procedure prescribed by the Juvenile Court Act in that they failed to notify the parents of the child and the Juvenile Court itself, that petitioner was deprived of his liberty for about a week without a determination of probable cause which would have been required in the case of an adult, that he was interrogated by the police in the absence of counsel or a parent, without warning of his right to remain silent or advice as to his right to counsel, that petitioner, while unlawfully detained, was fingerprinted in violation of the asserted intent of the Juvenile Court Act and that the fingerprints were unlawfully used in the District Court proceedings.[25]

U.S. Supreme Court's Decision.   The U.S. Supreme Court held that the Juvenile Court order waiving jurisdiction and remitting petitioner for trial in the District Court was invalid. The court said that the Juvenile Court's latitude in determining whether to waive jurisdiction is not without legal restraints, and held that the Juvenile Court must satisfy the basic requirements of due process and fairness and must comply with the statutory requirement of "full investigation." The *parens patriae* philosophy of the Juvenile Court is not an invitation to arbitrariness. The U.S. Supreme Court observed that the statute did not authorize the Juvenile Court, in total disregard of a motion for hearing filed by counsel, and without any hearing or statement or reasons, to decide that the child would be taken from the Receiving Home for Children, transferred to jail along with adults and be exposed to the possibility of a death sentence instead of treatment for a maximum, in Kent's case, of five years or until he was 21.[26] The judges lamented the fact that the Juvenile Court was neither able to deliver rehabilitative services to youth, nor able to give them their legal rights during trial. The children, as such, were getting a raw deal on both counts.

The court indicated there was substantial evidence that some juvenile courts lacked the personnel, facilities, and techniques to perform adequately as representatives of the State in a *parens patriae* capacity, at least with respect to children charged with law violation. The court expressed the belief that there were grounds for concern that the child receives the worst of both worlds: that he receives neither the protection accorded to adults nor the solicitous care and regenerative treatment postulated for children.[27]

In re GAULT et al.[28]

Brief Facts.   On June 8, 1964, Gerald F. Gault, age 15, and a friend, Ronald Lewis, were taken into custody by the Sheriff of Gila County, Arizona. The police action was taken as the result of a verbal complaint by the boys' neighbor, Mrs. Cook, concerning a telephone call made to her in which the caller or callers made lewd or indecent remarks. It was alleged that the contents of the call were of the irritatingly offensive, adolescent, sexual variety. At the time Gerald was picked up, his mother was at work and his father was out of town. On her return from work, Gerald's mother went to the detention home where Deputy Probation Officer Flagg, who was also superintendent of the detention home, told Mrs.

Gault "why Jerry was there." The probation officer said that a hearing would be held in juvenile court the following day.

Officer Flagg filed a petition with the court on the hearing day. It was not served on the Gaults. Mrs. Cook, the complainant, was not present at the hearing. No one was sworn, and no transcript or recording was made. At a subsequent hearing on June 15, the judge committed Gerald to the state industrial school as a juvenile delinquent, "for the period of his minority" (that is, until age 21), unless sooner discharged by due process of law. Arizona law did not permit appeals in juvenile cases.

The use of vulgar, abusive, or obscene language in the presence of or hearing of a woman or child is a misdemeanor according to the Arizona Criminal Code. The penalty specified in the criminal code, which would apply to an adult, was a fine of $5 to $50 or imprisonment for not more than two months. For the same offense, Gerald Gault (who was already under a six-month probation order at the time of the alleged phone call) was ordered to be committed to an institution for a period of about six years.

Grounds for the Petition. In August, 1964, a petition for a writ of habeas corpus was filed with the Supreme Court of Arizona. It was dismissed. The Gaults took the matter to the Supreme Court of the United States, challenging the validity of the juvenile code of Arizona on its face or as applied in this case. They contended that, contrary to the due process clause of the Fourteenth Amendment, the juvenile was denied the following basic rights when he was taken from the custody of his parents and committed to a state institution:

1. Notice of the charges.
2. Right to counsel.
3. Right to confrontation and cross-examination.
4. Privilege against self-incrimination.
5. Right to a transcript of the proceedings.
6. Right to appellate review.

Supreme Court's Comments. Although fully appreciating the historic intent, philosophy, and benevolent practices of the juvenile courts, the Supreme Court criticized the omission of due process of law. The judges stressed that procedure is an essential ingredient of law, and that only through due process is it possible for the truth to emerge. The Supreme Court noted that a juvenile court's unbridled discretion, however benevolently motivated, is frequently a poor substitute for principle and procedure. The Court concluded that the paternal advice of a juvenile court judge could be seen by a youth as very unfair when it is devoid of procedure, and emphasized the necessity for fairness, impartiality, and orderliness in juvenile court procedures. The court determined that the essentials of due process could be more impressive and more therapeutic to youth than the paternal approach of the juvenile court.

The court also suggested that due process of law is the primary and indispensable foundation of individual freedom. Emphasizing the need for legal procedure, the judges remarked that "the history of American freedom is, in no small measure, the history of procedure."[29]

According to the Supreme Court judges, the meaning of *parens patriae* is murky, and its historic credentials are of dubious nature. Furthermore, there is no trace of the doctrine in the history of criminal jurisprudence.[30] The doctrine of *parens patriae* recognized the child's right to custody, but not to liberty. Referring to a study conducted by sociologists Wheeler and Cottrell, the Court observed that when the procedural laxness of the "*parens patriae*" attitude is followed by stern disciplining, the contrast may have an adverse effect upon the child, who feels that he has been deceived or enticed.[31]

JAILING, DETAINING, AND INSTITUTIONAL COMMITMENTS

Far Too Many Juveniles are Jailed and Detained

Pending the disposition of their cases, some juveniles are kept temporarily in detention centers and youth shelters, but unfortunately, many others are sent to adult jails.[32] No accurate account of the extent of juvenile jailing in the United States exists at this writing. According to the National Jail Census conducted by the Department of Justice in 1970, there were 7,800 juveniles reported in 4,037 American jails on a given day in March, 1970.[33] These figures did not include the number of juveniles held in police lockups or "drunk tanks," but applied to the juveniles confined in a jail on any *one day*. The total number of juveniles processed through American jails in *one year* ran up to 500,000. This estimate was made in the mid-1970s. Although 67% of the juveniles confined in jails were awaiting trial, others were kept in jails pending their transfer to other institutions; a small number of them, most disappointingly, were serving their short sentences of one year or less. It was argued that there was no other alternative available for them. Despite the protests against jailing juveniles, significant numbers of them are being held in jails and their number is not decreasing.[34]

Who is Jailed?

One would expect that only dangerous delinquents are jailed. This is not the case. According to a survey conducted by the National Council of Crime and Delinquency (1971), 43% of children held in local jails were allegedly "persons in need of supervision."[35] These children apparently did not pose any threat to society, but did need some services. Females are more likely to be held for status offenses and also detained for a longer period of time than males. Jailed juveniles are generally poor and undereducated. Some judges prefer to jail youth, rather than using other less drastic alternatives, in order to "teach them a lesson."[36]

Incarcerating children in adult jails becomes more revolting when one comes to think of living conditions in jails. American jails are notorious for their woeful lack of basic necessities for physical and mental health. In many states, jails are under fire for not meeting minimal public health requirements. Sanitary conditions, food, exercise facilities, and means of fire control fall short of standards. The 1970 National Jail Census revealed that 86% of jails had no recreational facilities, about one-half of the jails had no medical facilities, and 5% of the jails are overcrowded.[37] Overcrowded jails breed more abuses among the inmates, such as fighting, bullying, and homosexual attacks, especially on younger and weaker inmates. Jail keepers are generally untrained in administering closed facilities, and do not have any long-range interest in acquiring the requisite training in the management of jails. They are usually on a temporary appointment. Every now and then, a case of youth molestation in jail surfaces, but many cases remain hidden. There have also been cases of fires in jails where many prisoners were burned to death.

Youths in Detention Centers

Detention centers have been created to avoid jailing youths in adult jails. Although detention centers and youth shelters have

Table 2.3. Number of Juvenile Detention and Correctional Facilities--United States, Midyear 1971, 1973, 1974 and 1975

Type of Facility	Number of Facilities				% Change 1971-75
	1971	1973	1974	1975	
All facilities	722	794	829	874	+21
Detention center	305	319	331	347	+14
Shelter	17	19	21	23	+35
Reception or diagnostic center	16	17	19	17	+6
Training school	191	187	185	189	-1
Ranch, forestry camp, and farm	115	103	107	103	-10
Halfway house and group home	78	149	166	195	+150

Source: U.S. Department of Justice, Children in Custody, 1975, Law Enforcement Assistance Administration, Washington, D.C., 1977.

Table 2.4. Juveniles Held in Public Juvenile Detention and Correctional Facilities, by Type of Facility--United States, Midyear 1971, 1973, 1974, and 1975.

Type of Facility	Number of Juveniles				% Change 1971-75
	1971	1973	1974	1975	
All facilities	54,729	45,694	44,922	46,980	-14
Detention center	11,767	10,782	11,010	11,089	-6
Shelter	360	190	180	200	-44
Reception or diagnostic center	2,153	1,734	1,376	1,436	-33
Training center	34,005	26,427	25,397	26,748	-21
Ranch, forestry camp, and farm	5,471	4,959	5,232	5,385	-2
Halfway house and group home	973	1,602	1,727	2,122	+118

Source: U.S. Department of Justice, Children in Custody, 1975, Law Enforcement Assistance Administration, Washington, D.C., 1977.

been in demand, their growth has been minimal during the first half of the 1970s, as evidenced in Table 2.3. Table 2.4 shows the trends in juvenile population held in various juvenile facilities.

Although it is heartening to find an overall decline in juvenile population in custodial institutions from 1971 to 1974, it is ominous to see an upward trend in 1975. However, the shift of youths from secure institutions to halfway houses and group homes is a clear trend to community-based treatment. Furthermore, there seems to be less reliance on the use of institutions for status offenders.

When we consider the total number of youths who pass through detention facilities annually, the number assumes large proportions. A total of 531,686 juveniles were admitted in 1971 to all types of temporary care facilities (shelters, diagnostic centers, and detention centers).[38] When added to the approximately 500,000 youths placed in jails each year, the number of youth committed to jails and detention centers exceeds one million. This is a shocking revelation of the magnitude of the problem. Sarri contends:[39]

> For every *ten* youth incarcerated in all types of residential correctional units, *nine* are held in jail or detention, and only *one* is held in all other types combined. Some might argue that detention must have a deterrent effect since so few youth go on into other types of correctional programs. However, negative experiences reported by so many youth raise serious questions about the use of jail and detention where it is not clearly required for protecting the community. Until the LEAA census data were available, one could plead ignorance of the magnitude of the problem. Now, the facts demand our active attention.

Sarri goes on to say that rates of detention in the United States generally exceed those of other industrialized nations for which data are available.[40] States differ greatly in their rates of jailing and detaining youth, and each state shows wide variations in its rates for counties. In one eastern state, jailing and detention rates among counties ranged up to 79% of all youths apprehended, with an overall average of 32%. Each county seems to have a certain tradition and an attitude toward jailing and detaining youths. Sarri concludes:[41]

> Lack of resources, lack of effort to develop alternatives, inappropriate responses to rising crime rates, lack of accountability by decision-makers, and last but not least, lack of adequate information systems that could monitor the jailing and detention processes, all contribute to the persistent use of frequent and unnecessary incarceration.

Some jailing and detaining is primarily for the convenience of the family or school or to reinforce the traditional views of controlling juveniles.[42]

Who is Detained?

The typical detainee is a male, with a median age of 14.7 years, who resides in a metropolitan area. About 25% of the males and 75% of the females are held for status offenses, for which

incarceration is hardly necessary. Blacks and minorities are detained more frequently than whites, as are juveniles from broken homes and those with prior records.[43]
The only justifications for detaining juveniles are:

1. That they may abscond before a court hearing.
2. They may commit a dangerous offense before court disposition.

These justifications are belied by the fact that only 2.7% of the juveniles fail to appear; very few of the juveniles detained are dangerous.[44] Fifty percent of the adjudicated delinquents and PINS (persons in need of supervision) are either status offenders or misdemeanants.[45]

Detention Staff

Although detention center staffs are generally of better quality than jail staffs, they are deficient in many respects. Professional workers are employed on a part-time basis or perform tasks in detention units as a result of volunteer work or employment with another agency. Most units do not have a sufficient number of well-trained supervisory staff, and about one-half of these units do not devote enough hours to in-service training. As a result, there is a greater emphasis on custody with all the attending negative influences. The untrained or ill-trained staff is neither able to provide the needed services to youth inside the centers, nor does it refer the inmates to community services outside the center. A large majority of detention unit directors admit they are forced to serve children who do not belong in a detention center. As many as 71% of such directors have reported that some youth they are asked to detain could be better served in foster homes. Unfortunately, there is a dearth of appropriate foster homes.[46]
In summary, youth in detention are typically in their early adolescence, are generally not dangerous (half of them being status offenders and misdemeanants) and are severed from the

community services which they direly need. The only redeeming feature is that the average length of stay for a youth in a detention home is about two weeks.

Commitment to Training Schools

A look at Tables 2.3 and 2.4 reveals that the number of training schools in the first half of the 1970s has remained about the same with 191 in 1971 and 189 in 1975. The number of juveniles held in training centers has declined somewhat. Many juveniles are now being diverted to halfway houses and group homes (Table 2.4). It appears that there is a growing realization of the futility of keeping large numbers of juveniles in training schools. However, there were 26,748 juveniles confined in training schools in the United States on June 30, 1975. This was the population on one day in these institutions; the total number of youth admitted to training schools annually is much greater.

Juvenile institutions have a history of skepticism, disappointment, and failure from their very inception. As has been stated previously, the earliest juvenile institution, known as a House of Refuge, was founded by New York philanthropists in 1825. Several states had Houses of Refuge by 1850. These houses were designed to be places of strict discipline, orderliness, and obedience. Children were kept under unrelenting supervision until they were reduced to a state of "cheerful submission." Critics alleged that these Houses of Refuge were as bad as the penitentiaries. During the era of reform in the last part of the 19th century, these Houses of Refuge came to be known as reform schools. With the growth in industry, these institutions started some trades for the youth and assumed the name of industrial schools. Later on, they were called training schools. The labels have been changed, but there has been little change in the program content of many of these institutions. To the harsh, repressive, disciplinary approach have been added industrial, educational, and religious programs. Juvenile institutions have failed to reduce delinquency. Recidivism rates remain notoriously high.

Decriminalization: A Response to Overcriminalization

The Juvenile Justice System and Status Offenders
Characteristics of Status Offenders
Rationales for Eliminating Status Offenses From Juvenile Court Jurisdiction
Responses to Arguments Favoring Retention of Status Offenses Under Court Jurisdiction
Recommended Approaches to Effect the Decriminalization of Status Offenses

Chapter 3

DECRIMINALIZATION

A Response to
Overcriminalization

THE JUVENILE JUSTICE SYSTEM AND STATUS OFFENDERS

A report[1] presented at the 1973 hearings of the House of
Representatives Select Committee on Crime by Dr. Rosemary
Sarri, Co-Director of the National Assessment of Juvenile Correc-
tions at the University of Michigan, stated:

> Perhaps the juvenile code provisions that result in the greatest
> miscarriage of justice are those which define the areas of behavior
> that the juvenile court may regulate. All 51 jurisdictions bring into
> the purview of the court conduct that, if engaged in by an adult,
> would bring legal action. But, in addition, all the states also permit
> the court to intervene with behavior that is not illegal for adults—
> i.e., truancy, incorrigibility, running away, immorality, disobedi-
> ence, promiscuity, or even just "idling." While all states have status
> offenses, as these latter behaviors are usually termed, there is
> considerable variation as to how they are treated. Recently, many
> states have adopted special legislation governing the processing of
> these "children in need of supervision" (CINS). Twenty-six states
> now have special categories for these juveniles, many of which

require that they be referred for service *outside* the juvenile justice system—i.e., the state social services department. It is debatable, however, whether these provisions are sufficient to divert youth from the system, because there is often some way of transforming them from status offenders to delinquents after the second or third such misbehavior. In one state with a separate category for status offenders, 80 percent of the institutionalized girls were truants, runaways, or ungovernables. In another state nearly 70 percent of all institutionalized girls were status offenders. Furthermore, it is not unusual to observe that females have longer periods of institutionalization than male juveniles who have committed more serious offenses.

Overreach of the law and overuse of criminal sanctions continue in many states despite their relative ineffectiveness in achieving the goals desired and in spite of the fact that they tend to have negative secondary and tertiary consequences. Many years ago Roscoe Pound expressed grave reservations over the extent to which the education, health, and morals of youth have come under the jurisdiction of the juvenile court. When these problems are written into statutes as bases for state intervention, parents, neighbors, schools, and social agencies are encouraged to avoid or refer their problems rather than to try to solve them.

Many students of juvenile justice have also recommended decriminalization not only of status offenses, but also of victimless crimes. In few states, however, have we observed any concerted drive in this direction for juveniles. In fact, there is some evidence that far more is being accomplished in decriminalization of behavior for adults than for juveniles, when a convincing argument could be made that decriminalization is even more urgently needed for juveniles. The objective of the system must be to minimize negative labelling, overuse of criminal sanctions, and intensification of state intervention.

Although no state has decriminalized status offenses, some important groups have advocated this type of juvenile code revision. In 1967, the President's Crime Commission reported that serious consideration, at the least, should be given to complete elimination of juvenile court jurisdiction over status offenses.[2] In 1974, the U.S. Congress ratified the National Juvenile Justice and Delinquency Prevention Act which mandated the removal of status offenders from jails, detention centers, and juvenile correctional institutions. In 1975, the Board of Directors of the National Council on Crime and Delinquency adopted a policy statement which advocated the removal of status offenses from juvenile court jurisdiction[3] and in 1976, the National Association of Counties, an organization which represents county governmental units in the United States, approved a resolution recommending that status offenses be eliminated from the jurisdiction of the juvenile court.[4] In 1980, Irving Kaufman, Chief Judge of the Second U.S. Circuit Court of Appeals, and chairman of the joint Institute of Judicial Administration/American Bar Association Commission on Juvenile Justice Standards, recommended the approval of "noncriminal behavior," the last and most controversial of 21 volumes of juvenile justice reforms. This reform advocated the removal of status offenses from juvenile court jurisdiction. Although the ABA House of Delegates deferred action on this standard, the authors anticipate favorable action on this standard by this body within a few years.

The National Assessment of Juvenile Corrections, University of Michigan found that status offenses comprise about 40% of the referrals to juvenile court.[5] The National Council on Crime and Delinquency reported that each year in the United States approximately 200,000 status offenders are held in secure detention pending a court hearing. Among the more than 85,000 children who are incarcerated annually in juvenile correctional institutions, 23% of the boys and 70% of the girls were adjudicated status offenders.[6] It should be noted that implementation of the federal Juvenile Justice and Delinquency Prevention Act has effected a decrease in the number of status offenders incarcerated in juvenile correctional institutions.

Status offenses as defined in juvenile statutes are often vague, lack clarity and specificity, and require judges or, at the very least, encourage them to exercise wide discretion in the application of highly subjective standards. For example, a California statute provides that a child under the age of 18 who habitually disobeys the proper orders of his parents or guardian, or who is a truant or "who from any cause is in danger of leading an idle, dissolute, lewd, or immoral life," comes under the jurisdiction of the juvenile court.[7] The National Assessment of Juvenile Corrections also found that juvenile codes provide juvenile court judges almost complete discretion in determining when and how to intervene in the lives of youth and that such interventions are often based on personal and professional belief systems, moral commitments, perceptions of community sentiments and administrative convenience.[8]

CHARACTERISTICS OF STATUS OFFENDERS

Stumphauzer stated that a person's behavior is inadequate or deficient in reference to some specific task or situation. Inadequacy of behavior, therefore, relates both to the available skills possessed by the individual and also to the complexity and demands of the situation (environment) in which he/she has to function.[9] Following are descriptions of skill deficiencies and complex, adverse environments which were experienced by a number of residents of a large southern city w.10 were placed on probation, detained in a detention center, or incarcerated in a juvenile correctional institution because they committed a status offense(s).

Case

Rhonda is 15, a ninth-grade student and the mother of a one-year old baby. Her grandmother filed a juvenile petition alleging that Rhonda dates an older boy and, on occasion, stays out overnight while in his companay. The petition also states that Rhonda does not properly care for her baby.

When Rhonda was four, the court declared her mother to be an "unfit parent." Rhonda was subsequently placed in the custody of her grandparents. She resides with her grandparents, who are in their seventies, and her younger brother, who is a homosexual.

Her natural father is deceased and her older brother is in jail. Her grandfather, who is an alcoholic, frequently becomes violent when intoxicated. On numerous occasions he has threatened Rhonda and other members of the family with his knife. The grandmother is currently seeking to have the grandfather removed from the home.

Case

Kenny is 14 and in eighth grade. He lives with his mother and her boyfriend. His mother's boyfriend, who is 10 years younger than Kenny's mother, frequently seeks to discipline Kenny by hitting him with his fists. Kenny's mother holds two jobs and spends most of her free time with her boyfriend. Kenny dislikes his mother's boyfriend and tries to avoid him whenever possible. Kenny's mother filed a petition against him alleging that he refuses to abide by her 10:00 P.M. curfew.

Case

Becky is 14 and in eighth grade. Her mother filed a petition alleging that Becky stayed away from home for three or four days without her permission, and that Becky is frequently truant from school. Becky lives with her mother and her mother's boyfriend. She resents her mother's boyfriend's attempts to discipline her. Her mother spends most of her free time involved in recreational activities with her boyfriend. Becky's mother often informs her that everyone would be better off if Becky were not in the home. Becky, who reads at the fourth grade level, attends school infrequently.

Case

Cindy is 15 and in tenth grade. Her mother filed a petition alleging that she frequently stays away from home overnight without parental permission. Cindy lives with her mother and a younger brother. Her father died when she was eight. Her mother's second marriage ended in divorce. Her mother often has emotional outbursts in which she screams and hits Cindy and her brother. On two occasions, Cindy has received medical attention for injuries inflicted upon her by her mother during these emotional outrages. It is not unusual for Cindy's mother to tell her to leave home and never return. Cindy is a good student and attends school regularly.

Case

A social worker filed a petition alleging that Duane, who is 12 and in sixth grade, has been truant from school. Duane, who is a diabetic, reads at the first-grade level. He lives in a low-income housing project with his mother, three brothers, and his mother's boyfriend. The housing project is in a high crime area. When Duane was 11, he was sexually assaulted while playing in his neighborhood. Police suspect that Duane's mother's boyfriend is a drug pusher. Duane's mother works the night shift. Although she voices concern that Duane is frequently absent from school, she is unwilling to take actions to see that he gets up in the morning or to confer with school personnel about his numerous absences from school. She is generally unaware of Duane's whereabouts.

Case

Debra is 14 and in eighth grade. A school social worker filed a petition alleging that she is truant from school. When Debra was eight, the juvenile court found her to be a neglected child, removed her from the custody of her mother and placed her in the custody of the Department of Social Services. When she was 10, the court, at the request of the Social Services Department, returned Debra to the custody of her mother. Because of limited funds and alcoholism, her mother is unable to keep a job. Debra lived with four different families during the 12 months preceding the filing of the truancy petition. Debra, who presently resides with a 20 year old woman, is not aware of where her mother currently resides.

Case

James is 11 and in fifth grade. He lives with his mother, four brothers, and one sister. His mother recently returned from prison. While she was incarcerated, the Department of Social Services had custody of the children. James' mother, who does not hold a job, states she is on the verge of having a nervous breakdown. She administers physical punishment to all the children on a frequent basis. As James is the oldest child, she expects him to help her perform household tasks. She filed a petition alleging that James stays away from home for extended periods of time without her permission.

Case

Diane is 14 and in eighth grade. During the past two years, Diane resided with her grandmother. At present she lives with her mother, sister, brother, and her mother's boyfriend. The boyfriend makes sexual advances toward Diane when her mother is absent from the home. She informed her mother about the conduct of the boyfriend; however, the mother did not believe her. Diane, who reads at the second grade level, is frequently absent from school. Her mother filed a petition against her alleging that she stayed away from home for two weeks without her permission.

Case

Rocky is 14 and in eighth grade. Rocky's parents were recently separated. He lives with his mother and three younger brothers. His mother, who is pregnant, is very concerned about her economic survival. She expects Rocky to function as the man of the house and berates him when he fails to meet her expectations. Rocky dislikes his father. His father has previously physically assaulted both Rocky and his mother with his fists. Recently, Rocky's mother allowed his father to move back into the home. Rocky subsequently left home for two weeks. While away from home, he stayed with friends. Rocky's father filed a petition alleging him to be a runaway.

Case

Barbara, a shy, short, very slender 15 year old, is in tenth grade. She lives with her mother. She does not know who her father is. Barbara and her mother have lived in seven different states. Her mother, who is unemployed, has a number of boyfriends. These boyfriends frequently spend the night with Barbara's mother. When Barbara was 13, one of her mother's boyfriends sexually assaulted her. The mother took no legal action against the boyfriend. Barbara dates a 21-year old man. She has spent a number of weekends with this man at his apartment. Her mother filed a petition alleging that Barbara ran away from home and stayed with this man for five days.

Case

Susan is 15 and in ninth grade. Her mother and stepfather, with whom she resides, have serious marital problems. Her stepfather, who has a drinking problem, is jealous of Susan. He has told the mother to choose either him or Susan. Both the mother and stepfather have physically abused Susan. When Susan was 14, school officials requested the Social Services Department to conduct an investigation because Susan's mother had inflicted numerous bruises on Susan's arms and back. As a result of this investigation, Susan was removed from the home for two months. Susan's mother filed a petition alleging that Susan refuses to comply with her requests.

Case

Jamie is 15 and in eighth grade. His mother filed a petition alleging that he stays away from home without her permission and is frequently truant from school. Jamie lives in a trailer park with his mother and her boyfriend. The boyfriend resents Jamie being in the home. Jamie frequently stays away from home without parental permission. He can usually be found at the home of a relative who also resides in the trailer park. Jamie's mother has moved four times during the past two years. Jamie, who reads at the second grade level, has been enrolled in six different schools during the past three years.

Case

Julie, a very intelligent, attractive ninth grader, is 15 years old. Julie lives with her 35-year old mother, a 19-year old stepfather and her sister, who is 17 years of age. Both Julie and her sister have had sexual relations with their stepfather. Her mother is jealous of both her daughters, and Julie and her sister are aware of this fact. Recently, Julie left home and moved in with two male college students. Her mother filed a petition alleging that she was a runaway.

Case

Joey is 14 and in eighth grade. When Joey was 10, his parents were divorced. Both parents have remarried. During the past four years, Joey has lived with both his natural parents. Neither parent wants to assume responsibility for caring for him, and he is aware of their feelings. At present Joey resides with his mother and stepfather. His stepfather is an unemployed alcoholic and has physically abused both Joey and his mother on a number of occasions. Six months ago, Joey's mother left home and went to live with her daughter. She informed Joey that she did not want him to accompany her. During her absence, Joey stayed away from home for extended periods of time. Recently, his mother returned to live with him and his stepfather. Joey dislikes his stepfather. For the past year, Joey has refrained from coming home until he thinks everyone is in bed. His mother filed a petition alleging that Joey uses abusive language toward her and his step-father and refuses to return home at times she designates.

Discussion

It is apparent that those youths described in the foregoing cases are extremely vulnerable. Unfortunately, most youths who penetrate the juvenile justice system for committing a status offense possess skill deficiencies and are exposed to home and school environments which greatly influence their behavior. Once a youth is adjudicated a status offender, the juvenile court requires him/her to immediately begin attending school on a regular basis, to come home at a designated time each night, and to comply with all requests of his parents, or face being detained in a detention center or jail or incarceration in a correctional institution. *All* responsibility for behavior change is placed on the youth. When one considers the capability of status offenders to immediately remediate their long-standing academic and social skill deficiencies and to control their home and school environments, it is not surprising that so many of these youths fail to comply with requirements of probation and, as a result, become deeply involved in the juvenile justice system.

RATIONALES FOR ELIMINATING STATUS OFFENSES FROM JUVENILE COURT JURISDICTION

After reviewing numerous studies of juvenile delinquency, the National Association of Counties Research Foundation and the National Assessment of Juvenile Corrections at the University of Michigan concluded:
1.   No evidence has yet been produced that juvenile detention and probation prevents or controls delinquency.[10]
2.   Legal processing and sanctions do not have a deterrent effect on the subsequent criminal behavior of youths. The earlier

youths are processed and the more stringent the sanction, the more likely it is that a youth will subsequently report or be processed for more frequent and more serious criminal law violations.[11]

Both the National Association of Counties Research Foundation and the National Assessment of Juvenile Corrections reviewed a cohort study of about 10,000 boys in Philadelphia by Figlio, Sellin, & Wolfgang. A major finding of this significant study was that boys who received punitive treatment (fines, probation, institutionalization) were more likely to violate laws and commit more serious offenses with greater rapidity than those who had less constraining contact with the system. Figlio et al. concluded that the juvenile justice system, at its best, has no effect on subsequent behavior and, at its worst, has a deleterious effect on future behavior.[12]

Findings of the National Assessment of Juvenile Corrections concerning the juvenile justice system and status offenses were:

1. Juvenile courts possess neither the expertise nor the resources to help children who commit status offenses. In fact, the majority of the respondents in a national survey agree that these problems are more appropriately handled by social service agencies. It seems reasonable to conclude that 40% or more of the cases referred to juvenile courts should not have been referred there in the first place. This is a rather onerous mishandling of "juvenile nuisances" with inestimable social costs. Consider, for example, the social and psychological costs of detention and institutionalization of status offenders by the courts, when it has been aptly demonstrated that such measures hardly have any ameliorative effects.[13]

2. The juvenile court's broad yet vague mandate over many juvenile problems enables it to become the "safety valve" for youth service agencies and parents. In particular, youth service agencies that want to protect their own domain, select the youth they wish to serve, reduce failures, and rid themselves of uncooperative youths, find the juvenile court a convenient agent to handle their "unwanted" cases. Once these referrals are made to the court,

youth service agencies and parents can wash their hands of responsibility to the youth involved. By its symbolic act of processing such a referral, the court in essence provides a legal certification that the referring parents and youth service agencies are not liable for the behavior of the youth and are absolved from responsibility if they fail to contain it. A major latent consequence of this role of the juvenile court is to reduce the pressure on youth service agencies, such as schools, child, and family service agencies, employment services, and mental health programs to respond more effectively to adolescence-related problems. Thus, for example, when children fail in school and are officially defined as delinquent because of behavior frequently resultant from such failure (i.e., truancy, incorrigibility), the schools are relieved from having to deal with the causes of the failure.[14]

3. Generally, children processed by juvenile courts are less likely to benefit from the services of other youth-serving agencies. The court itself is unlikely to call upon these agencies or to challenge their response to adjudicated juveniles. Nor is there any evidence to suggest that agencies are willing to serve such youths; rather, it seems that they prefer the court to assume responsibility for them. Children under court jurisdiction are likely to be thrust into a very narrow and limited pool of court services and be excluded from a wide variety of community youth services just at the time they need access to as many services as possible.[15]

Studies by Dixon[16] and Figlio et al.,[17] and Hasenfeld & Sarri's[18] review of juvenile delinquency studies, indicate that youth service programs that work are voluntary and youth who participate in programs under court orders, or under threat of incarceration if they fail, become more delinquent.

A study by the Ohio Youth Commission concluded that imprisonment of a status offender serves no humanitarian or rehabilitation purpose and is unwarranted and unjust punishment because it is disproportionate to the harm done by the child's noncriminal behavior.[19]

A national study conducted by Gold and Williams found that

children introduced into the juvenile court process become stigmatized and the benefits derived from such a classification for either the child or society appear to be nonexistent.[20] Although status offenses proscribed by statute are not applicable to criminal law, disposition seems to be viewed by the juvenile and general public as criminal sentencing. Vinter's national study of juvenile correctional programs found that 50% of all youth committed to these programs perceived themselves to be labeled as delinquent.[21]

Research findings by Sarri,[22] Wolfgang,[23] and Ferdinand and Luchterhand[24] reveal that the inclusion of status offenses within the jurisdiction of the juvenile court results in racial and economic discrimination in that a disproportionate number of children who are members of minority groups and who are poor tend to be referred to the juvenile court. Sarri also found that youth held in jail and detention are disproportionately selected from lower socioeconomic and minority populations, and are disproportionately charged with status offenses rather than felonies.[25] Numerous studies of hidden delinquency show that most juveniles commit an offense which could involve them in the juvenile justice system,[26] and studies of the characteristics of youth who penetrate the justice system, indicate that many youth from higher socioeconomic groups are able to avoid court processing.

A comparison of the percentage of boys (23%) and girls (70%) incarcerated in juvenile correctional institutions who are adjudicated status offenders indicates that girls who commit status offenses may be treated differently than boys by the justice system. Sarri found that females have a greater probability of being detained and held in jail for a longer period than males, even though the overwhelming majority of females are charged with status offenses.[27]

Based on the large number of youth who are referred to the juvenile court, detained in detention centers and jails, and incarcerated in juvenile correctional institutions, it seems evident that decriminalization of status offenses would effect significant reductions in the number of youth served by the justice system. Such reductions should make it possible for probation officers to provide more intensive supervision to youth who present a serious threat to persons and/or property, and for state and local governments to close a number of ineffective, expensive juvenile correctional institutions.

RESPONSES TO ARGUMENTS FAVORING RETENTION OF STATUS OFFENSES UNDER COURT JURISDICTION

It can generally be said that those groups which vehemently oppose decriminalization of status offenses will be affected by such a revision in juvenile codes. For example, juvenile court judges may lose power and prestige due to reductions in court staffs or because they are no longer able to intervene in the lives of a significant number of problem youth who reside in their communities. Juvenile probation officers, particularly those who primarily serve status offenders, may lose employment. School officials and social service department personnel will be held more accountable for providing more efficacious services to those youth who have serious home, school, and personal problems. Public and private child care institutions which primarily serve court referred status offenders, and depend on the court for payment for services provided to said youth, may lose a large amount of operating funds and staff. It seems clear that the aforesaid groups have a vested interest in retaining court jurisdiction over status offenses. Interestingly, these groups usually refrain from making comments about these vested interests. Rather, they promulgate arguments for maintaining court jurisdiction over status offenses which emphasize the important role the court plays in protecting and treating status offenders. Following are responses to those arguments most frequently articulated.

ARGUMENT. The use of legal sanctions against status offenders must be preserved as it is often necessary to force recalcitrant youth into treatment.

RESPONSE. Persons who employ this argument seem to make the following assumptions:

1. The juvenile court, through the threat of incarceration in a correctional institution, can force youths to utilize treatment services.
2. Treatment services youths need are available in the community, and the treatment services available will be beneficial to these youths.
3. Youths exert sufficient control of their behavior to eliminate those behaviors which brought them to the attention of the court.

These assumptions are not validated by research studies which show that the juvenile courts possess neither the expertise nor the resources to help youths who commit status offenses, that youths processed by the court are less likely to benefit from the services of agencies outside the justice system and youths who participate in programs under court orders, or under threat of incarceration if they fail, become more delinquent. It is more likely that a youth's participation in a treatment program is determined by the youth's perception of the quality of services provided by that program rather than an effort by the youth to avoid incarceration in a correctional institution. In other words, if a youth finds a program's services meaningful to him/her, he/she will probably utilize those services.

Residential and nonresidential services for which status offenders demonstrate the greatest need are usually not available in communities. Few communities have developed group home treatment units, specialized foster care services, emergency and temporary shelter care services, intensive counseling and casework services, and alternative remedial education programs in sufficient quantity and quality to meet the needs of youth who commit status offenses. Those programs available may refuse to provide services to status offenders. When agencies do make their services available to status offenders, these youths must rapidly adapt to these service programs or be rejected from the program, an event which often results in these youths becoming more deeply involved in the juvenile justice system.

The services to which status offenders are most frequently referred by the court are court probation departments and foster care services. Considering the quantity and quality of these services in most communities, it is questionable whether these services actually benefit youth.

Finally, those youths referred to the juvenile court for commiting a status offense are usually held accountable for immediately changing their inappropriate behavior. Unfortunately, skill deficiencies and environmental factors, which are beyond the control of these youths, but which significantly influence their behavior, may never be identified by the court. When such skill deficiencies and environmental factors are discovered by the court, the court rarely orders parents, school officials, or social service departments to alter their responses to these youths; even though, a change in their responses may be a necessary prerequisite to these youths having a reasonable opportunity to develop appropriate behaviors. It is, therefore, rather easy to understand why such a large number of status offenders experience a precipitious penetration into the juvenile justice system.

ARGUMENT.   Juvenile court jurisdiction over status offenses enables society to prevent serious delinquency by intervening early in the lives of youths who are exhibiting predelinquent behavior.

RESPONSE.   Thomas' examination of juvenile court records in two southern cities for a five-year period showed that a number of youths who initially appeared in juvenile court for a status offense reappeared in court for allegedly committing felonies a substantial number of times.[28] However, Clarke's analysis of the Philadelphia cohort study data of Figlio, Sellin, & Wolfgang not published in their book, *Delinquency in a Birth Cohort*,[12] indicated that the expectation of serious criminal activity of white boys in the cohort whose first offense was a status offense was about the same as for the entire population of white boys, including nonoffenders. Non-white boys who first appeared in court for a status offense had a much lower likelihood of serious delinquency than the white boys in the cohort.[29] Although it seems that, in some instances, the commission of a status offense may signal a risk of future serious delinquent behavior, research studies indicate that court intervention in the lives of those youth who commit status offenses may increase rather than reduce the likelihood of said youth engaging in serious criminal activity.[30]

ARGUMENT. Juvenile court jurisdiction over status offenses is required because some status offenders exhibit self-destructive behavior and present a potential threat to other persons or property to a degree that warrants their being placed on probation, detained in a detention center or jail, or incarcerated in a juvenile correctional institution.

RESPONSE. This argument has been used successfully to persuade state legislators that the juvenile court must have authority to intervene in the lives of status offenders. This argument is convincing because there are some status offenders who seem destined for total destruction to self and/or others unless someone with authority intervenes in their lives. Following is an example of such a case.

Case

Carolyn was a physically mature, attractive 14-year old who was in the seventh grade. She lived with her unemployed mother and four younger sisters. All the children had different natural fathers. Her mother refused to provide any of the children with needed supervision or discipline. Since age 13, Carolyn had earned money and clothes by giving sexual favors to older men. When she was at home, which was not often, she frequently threatened her mother and sisters with physical harm if they did not comply with her requests. Carolyn, who read at third-grade level, had been a chronic truant since the third grade. When she was not at school, she could usually be found in the company of a group of older youths. A substantial number of these youths had criminal records.

Opponents of decriminalization of status offenses could argue vociferously that the jurisdiction of the juvenile court should be invoked in this case for the purpose of securing Carolyn's attention, to let her know that she could not continue to exhibit self-destructive and inappropriate behaviors, and to provide her needed treatment services. The juvenile court did become involved with Carolyn. Following is a description of her experiences with the juvenile justice system:

Carolyn was 14 when her mother filed a petition against her, alleging that she was a runaway, truant, and out of parental control. As the mother seemed to be unaware of the whereabouts of her daughter, the juvenile court intake officer issued a detention order for Carolyn. One month later, the police apprehended Carolyn and placed her in the local detention center. Five days after her detention, Carolyn appeared in court for an adjudication hearing. She was adjudicated a status offender. The judge ordered that she be returned to the detention center for medical and psychological evaluations prior to his making a disposition of her case. Two weeks later, Carolyn returned to court for her disposition hearing. The judge placed her in the custody of the Department of Social Services (DSS) and ordered this agency to find Carolyn an appropriate placement outside of her natural home. Carolyn was also given a probationary status. Conditions of her probation were that she abide by the rules and regulations of DSS and not violate any state laws or local ordinances. After her disposition hearing, Carolyn was placed in a DSS emergency foster home. This home was supervised by houseparents who did not have specialized training in how to deal with problem youths. Eight other youths also resided in the home. One week after her placement in this home, Carolyn ran away. A DSS social worker immediately filed a petition against her and the juvenile court intake counselor issued a detention order. Two months later, the police apprehended Carolyn and placed her in detention. Five days later, she appeared in juvenile court. The judge found her to be delinquent in that she had violated the conditions of her probation, but informed her that she would be given another opportunity to adjust to foster care. After the court hearing, Carolyn was again placed in the same emergency foster home from which she initially ran away. Eight weeks after her second placement in the emergency foster home, Carolyn ran away again. The day before this, she and the female houseparent had a volatile argument concerning sexual advances which the houseparent accused Carolyn of making toward her husband.

During the two-month period that Carolyn resided in the emergency foster home, her DSS social worker talked with her on only three occasions. Carolyn did not have a probation officer because the juvenile court and DSS officials felt it would be a duplication of effort to have workers from both these departments delivering similar services to the same youth. In addition, Carolyn was not enrolled in a public school during the eight weeks she lived in the emergency foster home because DSS had a policy of not allowing youths in emergency foster homes to attend school. The rationale for this policy was that an emergency foster home placement was of such short duration that it would be disruptive for the youth, DSS, and the public schools for a youth to be admitted to a school when she may have to be withdrawn from the school once a permanent placement was found.

Carolyn's unauthorized departure from the emergency foster home resulted in another petition being filed by DSS and another detention order being issued by the juvenile court intake officer. Three months after said detention order was issued for Carolyn, police apprehended and detained her. Five days later, Carolyn, who was now 15, appeared in juvenile court. She was again adjudicated delinquent for violating conditions of her probation.

The judge reluctantly committed her to a juvenile correctional institution.

According to officials at the correctional institution, Carolyn was making an excellent adjustment to their program. They reported that she was complying with all the rules and regulations of the institution and was performing satisfactorily in academic and vocational classes.

They did not disclose that Carolyn had established a close relationship with a 16-year old girl who was incarcerated for prostitution and that Carolyn and her friend were engaging in sexual relations with a male staff member at the institution on a regular basis.

Twelve months after her admittance to the correctional institution, the correctional officials informed the juvenile court officials that Carolyn was ready for conditional release from the institution. The court officials regretfully informed the correctional officials that there was a shortage of foster homes and DSS officials did not feel they could place Carolyn in a permanent foster home. Both juvenile court and DSS officials recommended that Carolyn remain in the correctional institution until an appropriate placement could be found. Juvenile court and DSS officials agreed that Carolyn should not be returned to her natural home setting.

Six months later, correctional officials again apprised juvenile court officials that Carolyn could be given a conditional release from the institution. Officials of DSS and the court agreed that Carolyn should be removed from the institution, but DSS had not been able to identify a proper placement for her as there continued to be a serious shortage of foster homes, and private child care institutions were unwilling to admit a youth with a history like Carolyn's. Court and DSS officials finally concluded that Carolyn, now 17, should be able to adjust to her natural home setting. Carolyn returned to live with her mother and youngest sister. Her other three sisters were now incarcerated in juvenile correctional institutions.

Six months after her release from the correctional institution, Carolyn left home and moved to another city where she became employed as a masseuse in a massage parlor. When Carolyn was 18, she was arrested and convicted for prostitution. She was sentenced to six months in the county jail.

Discussion

Although most status offenders who penetrate the juvenile justice system are not in a predicament like Carolyn when they enter the system, many of these youths are victimized by ineffective, inhumane, and costly juvenile justice and foster care systems. Even though officials of these systems have good intentions when they become involved in the lives of these youths, these systems, as illustrated in Carolyn's case, often create more problems for the youth than they solve.

Although opponents of decriminalization of status offenses would assert that it was both appropriate and necessary for a petition to be filed against Carolyn, there were other options available to both Carolyn's mother and youth service agencies. However, the juvenile court, by having jurisdiction over status offenses, and by being willing to allow Carolyn's mother to dump Carolyn into the juvenile justice system, significantly reduced the chances that other options would be utilized. Some of the options which could have been used include, but are not necessarily limited to, the following:

1. Since Carolyn's mother was unaware of her whereabouts, she could have filed a Missing Person Report. Police have a responsibility to search for a missing person just as diligently as they do for a status offender for whom they have a detention order.

Police do not have to possess a detention order to hold a runaway for a brief period until a parent can come and get the youth. Most states grant broad authority to police officers to take juveniles into custody under circumstances in which they are, in the broadest sense, endangered by their surroundings.[31] Therefore, it is possible for police to "take a youth into custody" without "arresting" the youth. States which grant this discretion to police consider this to be a protective rather than a punitive form of detention.

Police will usually need a detention order if it is necessary for them to enter a private dwelling for the purpose of searching for a "runaway." However, if the police or a parent have reason to believe that a youth is being allowed to stay in a particular home, they can advise the residents of that home that they will be charged with contributing to the delinquency of a minor if they continue to permit the youth to stay in that home. Often this type of warning, particularly if stated forcefully by police officers, is sufficient to motivate the adults in the home to discontinue providing the youth shelter. This approach frequently eliminates one of the youth's primary alternatives to staying away from home.

2. Carolyn's mother could have filed a "dependent petition" stipulating that she was unable to provide Carolyn with proper supervision and care. Filing of the dependent petition would have provided the court an opportunity to remove Carolyn from the home without placing her in a position which increased her chances of becoming deeply involved in the juvenile justice system. If Carolyn had refused to appear in court at the time the dependent petition was considered, it may have been necessary to issue a detention order to secure her initial appearance in court; however, she would not have been subject to further involvement in the justice system because of her failure to appear in court.

3. Carolyn's mother could have requested DSS, the school social worker, or other youth service personnel to assist her to learn effective parenting skills.

4. Carolyn's mother could have, either directly or indirectly, informed the men who were purchasing sexual favors from Carolyn that they would be charged with contributing to the delinquency of a minor if they continued to sexually exploit Carolyn.

5. Since Carolyn's mother was clearly not providing her children with proper supervision or discipline, and Carolyn was in an environment injurious to her welfare, a school social worker,

who should have been involved with Carolyn because of her chronic school truancy, could have filed either a dependent or neglect petition. Neither of these types of juvenile petitions are filed *against* the youth, but simply allege that the youth is in a condition of dependency or neglect. These petitions can be filed in order to have the court determine the nature of the youth's condition and to take constructive action to help the youth. Most states do not authorize the commitment of a neglected or dependent youth unless the petition filed also alleges delinquency.

6.   Since Carolyn's mother was unwilling to take any action to influence her daughter to attend school, a school social worker could have filed a complaint alleging that Carolyn's mother was in violation of the compulsory school attendance law. This legal action would have allowed the court to place more responsibility on the mother for improving Carolyn's school attendance.

7.   When Carolyn ran away from the emergency foster home, DSS officials could have filed a Missing Person Report rather than filing a petition against her. This agency could also have possibly prevented Carolyn from running away if its officials had provided her with a foster care placement which met her special needs and had given her more counseling services while she resided in the emergency foster home.

8.   School officials could have probably motivated Carolyn to improve her school attendance if they had made a greater effort to place more responsibility on Carolyn's mother to get Carolyn to school and had offered Carolyn educational experiences which would have provided her an opportunity to remediate her significant academic skill deficiencies.

Granted, most of these options are not as administratively convenient as filing a petition alleging a youth to be a status offender and issuing a detention order for the youth. Furthermore, use of one or more of these options would not have necessarily precluded Carolyn from ultimately being sentenced to a jail term for prostitution. However, the benefits derived from using these options would have included, as a minimum, the following:

1.   Carolyn would have been removed from her adverse

home situation, if even for a brief period, without a petition being filed against her alleging the commission of a status offense.
2. Carolyn's mother would have a chance to learn needed parenting skills.
3. Pressure would have been placed on persons to refrain from contributing to Carolyn's problems, and thereby, manipulating Carolyn's environment in a positive manner.
4. The court could have ordered DSS to conduct an investigation to determine whether Carolyn's younger sisters needed to be removed from their home.
5. Rather than being allowed to transfer responsibility for Carolyn to the juvenile court, Carolyn's mother would have been held more accountable for providing Carolyn with the supervision and discipline required to effect improvement in her home and school attendance behavior.
6. School and DSS officials would have had to assume more responsibility for developing and delivering efficaciously those services most needed by Carolyn and other problem youths.
7. As Carolyn would not have been incarcerated in a correctional institution, the responses of the juvenile justice system toward her would have been more constructive, humane, and probably less costly to taxpayers.

ARGUMENT. Residential and nonresidential services for which status offenders demonstrate a dire need are not available in sufficient quantity or quality in communities; consequently, status offenses should remain under juvenile court jurisdiction until such time as these services are developed.

RESPONSE. Certainly few communities have developed the residential and nonresidential services which status offenders require. Proponents of decriminalization of status offenses would argue that the juvenile court, by retaining jurisdiction over status offenses, reduces the likelihood that these desperately needed services will ever be created. In an address to juvenile court judges, Judge David Bazelon, United States District Court of Appeals for the District of Columbia, supported this view when he stated:[32]

> The situation is truly ironic. The argument for retaining beyond-control and truancy jurisdiction is that juvenile courts have to act in such cases because "if we don't act, no one else will." I submit that precisely the opposite is the case: *because* you act, no one else does. Schools and public agencies refer their problem cases to you because you have jurisdiction, because you exercise it, and because you hold out promises that you can provide solutions.

Judge Bazelon's appraisal is accurate. It can generally be demonstrated that most communities are not inclined to appropriate funds to develop services needed by status offenders, especially status offenders with very serious problems, as long as communities can use the juvenile justice system to remove these youths "out of sight and out of mind."

This argument by opponents of decriminalization of status offenses is also based on the assumption that status offenders who have access to juvenile court services will be better off than those status offenders who are not provided such services. Empirical research does not support this assumption. As has been previously stated, the National Assessment of Juvenile Corrections found that children under court jurisdiction are likely to be thrust into a very narrow and limited pool of court services and be excluded from a wide variety of community youth services just at the time they need access to as many services as possible.

RECOMMENDED APPROACHES TO EFFECT THE DECRIMINALIZATION OF STATUS OFFENSES

Rationales previously elucidated for eliminating status offenses from juvenile court jurisdiction include:

1.   The juvenile court possesses neither the expertise nor the resources to help status offenders.

2. The detention, jailing, and incarceration of many status offenders increases the likelihood that these youths will commit more serious offenses.

3. The inclusion of status offenses under court jurisdiction results in racial, economic, and sex discrimination.

4. Court jurisdiction over status offenses enables parents and youth service agencies to use the court as a dumping ground for their "unwanted."

5. The vast amount of human and economic resources expended by the juvenile justice system to deal with status offenders should be used to provide services and intensive supervision to youths who present a serious threat to persons or property.

Although the foregoing rationales would seem sufficient to warrant a revision in juvenile codes, state legislatures have not been inclined to decriminalize status offenses. Some of the reasons why status offenses have remained under court jurisdiction are:

1. Youth advocacy groups concerned with improving juvenile justice have concentrated their efforts on establishing services which would preclude status offenders from being placed in detention centers and jails and incarcerated in juvenile correctional institutions rather than seeking the enactment of legislation which would decriminalize status offenses.

2. It is not the nature of organizations to relinquish power. The juvenile justice system, whether state or locally administered, is not an exception to this truism. The unwillingness of the justice system to relinquish power is demonstrated by the opposition of juvenile justice system personnel to the decriminalization of status offenses and the system's direct or indirect control over programs which have been created to keep status offenders away from the juvenile justice system.

3. Schools, social service departments, and other youth service agencies which rely on the juvenile court to handle youths who do not adapt to their programs have not supported decriminalization of status offenses. This lack of support is probably due to their realization that if they are no longer able to transfer responsibility for status offenders to the juvenile court, it will be necessary

for them to modify aspects of their programs which do not meet the needs of youth and to develop new, innovative programs.
4.   Because of economic considerations, the administration of juvenile corrections has moved almost entirely from the local to the state level. Local governments have not pressured state legislatures to decriminalize status offenses because they realize additional *local* tax dollars may have to be appropriated to finance the operation of services for which status offenders demonstrate a great need.

RECOMMENDATION: Local and state youth advocacy groups (see Chapter 7) should influence state legislatures to both decriminalize status offenses and allocate block grants of funds to local units of government for the purpose of developing and delivering locally identified and locally controlled community-based services for status offenders.

RECOMMENDATION: Although status offenses remain under court jurisdiction, local youth advocacy groups should persuade juvenile court judges to take actions to significantly reduce the number of youths who become involved in the juvenile justice system for committing a status offense. Some actions which a juvenile court judge can take to decrease the number of status offenders who penetrate the juvenile justice system are:

1.   Inform juvenile court intake officers that the court will only authorize detention orders for youths who have had a petition filed against them alleging the commission of an act that would be considered a crime if committed by an adult, and who present an imminent threat to other persons or property.
2.   Apprise juvenile court intake counselors that petitions filed against youths which include *only* status offenses will be dismissed forthwith unless the following actions have been taken by a prospective petitioner prior to a petition being filed:
    a.   Prospective petitioners must have exhausted all legal options prior to the filing of a petition alleging the commission of a status offense. These options may include filing a "depen-

dent petition" or "neglect petition," filing a missing person report, filing a complaint alleging that someone is contributing to the delinquency of the youth or filing a complaint charging a parent or guardian with violating the compulsory school attendance law, etc.

b. Prospective petitioners must document, as shown by the signatures of youth service personnel, that *all* possible services outside the juvenile justice system have been fully utilized to help the youth.

c. If the prospective petitioner is representing a youth service agency, he/she must specify the quantity of services which his agency has delivered to the youth and specify those services which the juvenile court has to offer which are likely to remediate the youth's behavior. In addition, he must delineate efforts made by his agency to identify environmental factors and skill deficiencies which may be influencing the youth's behavior.

The aforesaid actions would definitely reduce the number of status offenders who become involved in the juvenile justice system. However, it is unlikely that most judges will take such actions, unless, they are pressured to do so by influential youth advocacy groups.

Diversion: A Response to Overprocessing

What is Diversion?
Advancement of Diversion Practices/Programs
Delinquency Causation Theories Which Support Diversion
Rationales for Diversion
A Description of Diversion Practices/Programs
    Goals Established for Diversion Practices/Programs
    Organizational Dynamics of Diversion Practices/Programs
        Legal Structure
        Paralegal Structure
        Nonlegal Structure
    Diversion Practices/Programs Inside and Outside the Juvenile Justice System
Negative Consequences of Diversion Practices/Programs
Evaluations of Diversion Programs
A Description of Four Diversion Programs
    Sacramento Diversion Program
    Mecklenburg County Youth Services Bureau
    Philadelphia Neighborhood Youth Resources Center
    Urbana-Champaign Adolescent Diversion Project
Recommendations to Ameliorate Diversion Practices/Programs

Chapter 4

DIVERSION

A Response to Overprocessing

WHAT IS DIVERSION?

Diversion means many things to many different people. A recent study noted that the term diversion has been used to describe almost any discretionary action available to a public or private agency dealing with youth.[1] Following are definitions which have been promulgated for diversion:

1. Diversion is the channeling of cases to noncourt institutions in instances where these cases would ordinarily have received an adjudicatory or fact-finding hearing by the court. It should be distinguished from preventative efforts which contain no possibility that the juvenile's behavior would result in a court hearing.[2]

2. Diversion is any process employed by components of the juvenile justice system (police, prosecution, courts, corrections) to turn suspects and offenders away from the formal system, or to a lower level of the system.[3]

3.   Diversion occurs after a youth's official contact with an agent of the law and prior to formal adjudication.[4]

4.   Diversion is a process designed to reduce the further penetration of youth into the juvenile justice system. Diversion can occur at any point following apprehension by police for the alleged commission of a delinquent act and prior to adjudication.[5]

5.   Diversion is a referral of a juvenile to a community-based program or agency outside the juvenile justice system.[6]

6.   Diversion represents those activities by public officials such as police and intake and probation officers that result in direct referral of the juvenile to agencies and persons who are capable of handling the problem outside the jurisdiction of the juvenile justice system.[7]

7.   Diversion is an exercise of discretionary authority to substitute an informal disposition prior to a formal hearing on an alleged violation.[8]

8.   Diversion should be reserved to denote the channeling of youth away from the juvenile justice system at an early point. It should not be used to mean a different routing within the components of the juvenile justice system.[9]

The primary differences among the foregoing definitions of diversion seems to be the degree of legal authority or control the juvenile justice system exerts over a child during the diversion process.

In a national evaluation of diversion practices/programs McDermott concluded that there are two types of diversion practices, "true diversion" and "minimization of penetration." He defined the terms as follows:

1.   *True diversion* is a discretionary act directed at forestalling adjudication which results in a termination of official intervention and/or referral of a youth to a program outside the system.[10]

In the National Assessment of Juvenile Corrections (NAJC) exploratory study of diversion processes in juvenile justice, Cressey defined *true diversion* as occurring when a juvenile is safely out of the realm of the juvenile justice system and is immune from incurring the delinquent label or any of its variations. He also stated that the failure to provide a helping service is not considered a positive act of diversion.[11]

2. *Minimization of penetration* is a process which results in further system intervention and/or referral to a justice system program.[12]

McDermott reports that practitioners tend to interpret diversion as a minimization of penetration rather than as an end of further processing by the juvenile justice system. These persons seem to view the *intensity* and *degree* of processing to constitute the harm rather than the processing itself. In practice, diversion has come to mean a turning aside from formal processing (i.e., adjudication).[13]

It is clear that ambiguity surrounds the concept of diversion. McDermott suggests that policy makers must choose between true diversion and minimization of penetration. If the choice is true diversion, then support for traditional diversion processes within the juvenile justice system and support for diversion programs operated or controlled by the justice system must be withdrawn. If the choice is minimization of penetration, expansion of diversion programs developed within and controlled by legal authorities should be encouraged.[14]

ADVANCEMENT OF DIVERSION PRACTICES/PROGRAMS

Since 1967, a number of official bodies have supported the diversion of youth from the juvenile justice system.

The 1967 President's Crime Commission Report recommended the establishment of alternatives to the juvenile justice system. It was recommended that service agencies capable of dealing with certain categories of juveniles who routinely come into contact with the juvenile justice system should have juveniles diverted to them. This report stated:[15]

> The formal sanctioning system and pronouncement of delinquency should be used as a last resort. In place of the formal system,

dispositional alternatives to adjudication must be developed for
dealing with juveniles, including agencies to provide and coordinate services and procedures to achieve necessary control without
unnecessary stigma. Alternatives already available, such as those
related to court intake, should be more fully exploited.

During 1971–72, the International Association of Police
Chiefs conducted seven conferences for the purposes of assessing
current problems in the juvenile justice system and to determine
what measures had been taken to implement recommendations in
the President's 1967 Crime Commission Report. Three hundred
and fifty of the nation's leading authorities on youth were invited
to participate in these conferences.[16] One of the recommendations
made by conference participants was:[17]

Pre-adjudication diversion programs should be established in every
community and/or governmental jurisdiction under the auspices of
the community juvenile justice system to re-route juvenile offenders, particularly those who are charged with misdemeanors, status
offenses and first offenses, from the formal machinery of the
juvenile justice system, insofar as is warranted by the nature of the
individual case.

In 1973, the National Advisory Commission on Criminal
Justice Standards and Goals advocated that youth service bureaus
be established to focus on the special problems of youth in the
community. One rationale stated for this recommendation was to
meet the need for an alternative to juvenile court processing for
many youth.[18] This recommendation reinforced the 1967 President's Crime Commission's recommendation to establish a new
community agency to be known as a Youth Services Bureau, a
recommendation based on the premise that a substitute agency was
needed to effect the diversion of a substantial number of youth
from the juvenile justice system.

In 1974, the Federal Juvenile Justice and Delinquency Prevention Act was ratified. Under this act, funds have been appropri-

ated to state and local units of government for the purpose of establishing diversion programs.

In 1975, the Board of Directors, National Council on Crime and Delinquency, advocated the elimination of status offenses from juvenile court jurisdiction.[19] In 1976, the National Association of Counties, an organization which represents county governmental units in the United States, approved a resolution also recommending that status offenses be removed from the jurisdiction of the court.[20] A primary reason for this recommendation by these national organizations was to reduce the number of children inappropriately processed by the juvenile justice system.

In 1976, pursuant to the authority of the 1974 Federal Juvenile Justice and Delinquency Prevention Act, the Law Enforcement Assistance Administration provided $10 million for public and private agencies to develop innovative programs to divert juvenile offenders from the juvenile justice system. The purposes of this program were to design and implement demonstration projects which would develop and evaluate approaches to diverting youth from involvement in the traditional juvenile justice system at the critical points of penetration and to determine the significance of providing effective and coordinated services to a portion of those youth diverted. Specific alternatives to juvenile justice system processing which were outside the system, including provision of services and complete release, were emphasized.[21]

In 1976, the Law Enforcement Assistance Administration prepared its *First Comprehensive Plan for Federal Juvenile Delinquency Programs*. A major program objective stated in the plan was:[22]

> To lessen the inappropriate intervention of the juvenile justice system in the lives of youth by diverting appropriate juveniles from involvement with the juvenile justice system.

The stated rationale for this objective was to avoid negative labeling and stigmatization of youth and to focus limited justice system resources on those youth requiring such programming.

DELINQUENCY CAUSATION THEORIES WHICH SUPPORT DIVERSION

Labeling theory, as developed by Mead, Tannenbaum, Blumer, Lemert, Becker, and others, and *differential association theory*, as developed by Mead, Thomas, Blumer, Sutherland, Ohlin, Glaser, Short, Cohen, Matza, and others, are the primary delinquency causation theories which support the implementation of diversion practices/programs.

The basic contention of the labeling theory is that individuals stigmatized as delinquent become what they are said to be.[23] In other words, once a youth has been branded as a wrong-doer, it becomes extremely difficult for him/her to shed that identity. The case history or record stands in testimony to the youth's unworthiness.

Shur states that a stigmatizing experience often imposes new restrictions on limited opportunities and raises possibilities of future deviation.[24]

Lemert defines stigmatization as a process which assigns marks of moral inferiority to deviants and constitutes a form of degradation which transforms identities and status for the worse. Lemert asserts that further stigmatization is both implicit and explicit in formal court procedures. He supports this assertion with the following illustrations:[25]

1.   Intake interviews and those in subsequent investigations are often inquisitions seeking admissions of guilt or complicity in offenses.

2.   Detention means loss of freedom, removal of personal possessions, subjugation to arbitrary security rules and, in some juvenile halls, surveillance by microphones and closed circuit television.

3.   Court hearings often are degradation rituals in which probation officers recite in detail the moral failings or unfitness of

children, youth, and parents. Hostile witnesses augment the condemnations. Judges frequently deliver sermon-like lectures loaded with threats which confront children and parents with choices of reform or dire consequences. For emphasis, judges have been known to read incriminating facts or opinions from probation records during court hearings.

4. Contents of court and police records often become known. This can and does serve as a handicap in areas of employment and education.

Lemert points out furthermore that the aforedescribed degradation ritual has significant negative impact for some youth, but is absorbed or discounted by others.[25a] Shur supports Lemert's views concerning the impact of stigmatization when he states:[26]

> The labeling approach does not assert that the stigmatizing process is simple and direct or unvarying. It alerts us to the strong possibility that various kinds of interventions in the lives of children may have these effects; indeed that such interventions may do more harm than good.

Shur also believes that recent empirical research in which students' IQ scores and grades directly varied according to the nature of information provided to their teachers about the students' "prospects," documents that the labeling process is almost bound to have undesirable social-psychological side effects.[27]

It seems clear that proponents of the labeling theory believe the self-concepts and long-term behavior of youth who penetrate the juvenile justice system are vitally influenced by their interaction with this system.

The differential association theory holds that youth engage in delinquent behavior because they experience an overabundance of interactions, associations, and reinforcements with behavior patterns favorable to delinquency. Consequently, potential delinquents should not be cast into interaction with more experienced ones.[28] Support for this theory can be obtained from studies which document that, within an institutional setting, the delinquent peer group provides massive schedules of positive reinforcement for deviant behavior and punishment for socially conforming behavior. This finding indicates delinquent adolescents might be expected to provide an excellent opportunity for maintaining existing deviant behavior, and for the novice an opportunity to acquire new sets of deviant behavior.[29]

Although both the labeling and differential association theories of delinquency causation are generally highly regarded by academicians and juvenile justice practitioners, McDermott, in a national evaluation of juvenile diversion, concluded that the demonstrated diversion practices of practitioners who implement the diversion process indicate they are having extreme difficulty interpreting these theories.[30]

RATIONALES FOR DIVERSION

Numerous rationales are espoused favoring the implementation of diversion practices/programs. The National Assessment of Juvenile Corrections at the University of Michigan elucidated the following rationales for the effectuation of such practices/programs:

1. Research findings are consistently showing that legal processing and sanctions do not have a deterrent effect on subsequent criminal behavior. The earlier youths are processed and the more stringent the sanction, the more likely it is that a youth will subsequently report or be processed for more frequent and more serious law violations. Thus, if one wished to deter delinquent behavior, the findings would suggest a strategy of parsimony with respect to judicial intervention.[31]

2. Generally, children processed by the juvenile courts are less likely to benefit from the services of other youth service agencies. The court itself is unlikely to call upon these agencies or to challenge their response to adjudicated juveniles. Nor is there any evidence to suggest that agencies are willing to serve such youths; rather it seems that they prefer the court to assume responsibility for them. Children under court jurisdiction are likely to be

thrust into a very narrow and limited pool of court services and be excluded from a wide variety of community services just at the time they need access to as many services as possible.[32]

3.   The powers of the juvenile court are extraordinary and should be reserved for extraordinary, not minor, cases.

4.   Large numbers of cases interfere with optional functioning of the court, with the result that processing of cases is slow and highly bureaucratic.

5.   Juvenile courts have limited staff and monies. If they are overloaded, ineffectiveness will increase, and it will not be possible to concentrate on serious delinquency cases.

6.   The juvenile court was established as a court of law, and its limitations in remedying social ills must be accepted. It cannot order morality, make a child or a parent good, or induce respect for authority.[33]

7.   Juvenile courts possess neither the expertise nor resources to help children who commit status offenses. Approximately 40% of the children referred to the juvenile court are sent there for committing a status offense. Certainly this group of children should be diverted from the juvenile justice system.[34]

Three additional rationales frequently stated for diversion are:

1.   Diversion is a significantly less expensive method of attempting to solve the problem of juvenile delinquency (e.g., the Sacramento Diversion Project, see pp. 113-114, infra.).[35]

2.   Diversion is far more humane than formal processing in that the deprivations (e.g., detention, informal probation, etc.) incurred by youths who are processed are not encountered by diverted juveniles.[36]

3.   Diversion should be emphasized because delinquency is widespread among all segments of society. Delinquents are not basically different from non-delinquents. Furthermore, juveniles who penetrate the juvenile justice system seem to become more delinquent.[37]

Students of the juvenile justice system realize that diversion is inherent in the juvenile justice system and necessary to keep it from collapsing. Consequently, diversion will occur whether one is for or against it, for or against the juvenile justice system, or for or against extending constitutional protections to children. The question is not whether diversion should occur, but when and under what circumstances it is best encouraged.

A DESCRIPTION OF DIVERSION PRACTICES/PROGRAMS

This section lists goals established for diversion programs, describes the organizational dynamics of diversion practices/programs, and discusses diversion practices/programs inside and outside the juvenile justice system.

Goals Established for Diversion Practices/Programs

McDermott (1976) stated that the following goals are frequently established for diversion programs:[38]

1. To reduce stigma
2. To decrease the number of court cases
3. To decrease caseloads of court personnel
4. To deliver more effective, faster services
5. To free the juvenile court to handle more difficult cases
6. To increase efficiency in the delivery of juvenile justice
7. To reduce juvenile crime rates
8. To assist parents and youth to solve problems
9. To develop an advocacy role relative to youths

The strengths and weaknesses of the organizational milieu in which diversion programs operate determine whether diversion goals will be achieved. Regulations, rules, guidelines, and informal relationships that guide juvenile justice system personnel in their intra- and interagency interaction are crucial elements of an organizational milieu.[39]

Organizational Dynamics of Diversion Practices/Programs

McDermott reported that *legal, paralegal,* and *nonlegal* organizational structures are employed to implement diversion practices/programs.

LEGAL STRUCTURE.[40] This structure represents a minimization of penetration approach to diversion. Under this structure, the diversion program is administered by a functionary of a legitimate social control agency as part of his/her bureaucratic responsibility. Formal legal sanctions can be imposed. Coercion, whether implicit or explicit, maintains a strong presence in the program. Programmatic developments are administered and staffed by a social control agency and the program is physically located on or within the social control agency's official premises. The organizational context of the legal type of diversion is that of the official juvenile justice system, particularly the police or probation departments.

PARALEGAL STRUCTURE.[41] A diversion program under this structure is funded and administered or controlled by the juvenile justice system. It is staffed by system personnel (on loan or sabbatical leave) and has offices physically based with system offices. It has access to all juvenile records or allows the justice system access to its records. It receives clients by means of explicit coercion through the system and maintains an informal or formal system of reporting on progress of those juveniles served. A great deal of similarity or co-optation of the alternative by the official justice system is commonplace.

NONLEGAL STRUCTURE.[42] A diversion program under this structure is client-oriented. Client participation is voluntary. In fact, even implicit coercion is watched for and resisted. There is no sanction against clients for nonparticipation or termination of participation, and the juveniles served perceive the program as nonlegal. An advocacy role is acceptable. This program establishes goals independently without pressure from the funding source and maintains control over staff appointments. In order for a diversion program to be classified as nonlegal, its day to day practices must exhibit freedom from reliance upon legal authority and/or control by agents or agencies exercising legal authority. Present funding trends for diversion are in the direction of support for specialized programs of the legal or paralegal type. The result is tacit approval of minimization of penetration as a diversion practice.[43]

Diversion Practices/Programs Inside and Outside the Juvenile Justice System

The preceding section centered on the organizational context in which diversion practices/programs operate. This section will delineate those units inside and outside the juvenile justice system which implement diversion practices/programs.

Diversion practices/programs *inside* the system involve police and probation departments. In an exploratory study of diversion processes in juvenile justice, Cressey concluded that a policeman can divert youth *from* admission to the juvenile justice system, but a probation intake officer can only divert youth *out* of the system they have entered, or minimize their penetration in the system.[44]

As perhaps 80% of youths encountering the police are released without any formal processing or recording, it is clear that most diversion takes place at the police level.[45] Within the police department there may be a patrol officer, juvenile specialist unit, and/or school resource officer who, by doing something short of formal processing, engage in diversion practices. The *patrol officer* may cite, warn and release youth. Resistance to these procedures may result in official action. *Juvenile specialist units* usually view their tasks as diverting youths from probation (minimization of penetration). Juveniles may be counseled, warned, released, placed on informal probation, or referred to a private or public program. The *school resource officer* is normally assigned to a school. He/she may serve as a counselor, friend, lecturer, guard, and probation officer. It is important to note that the school resource officer is first a police officer, an official of the juvenile justice system. He may prevent youths from having contact with the system. Police may also operate diversion programs. These programs frequently emphasize counseling and/or recreational services to juveniles.[46]

Regardless of one's definition of diversion, probably 90% of all probation department diversion occurs as a result of actions taken by the probation intake officer.[47] Most youth come into contact with the probation department by means of police or parent referrals. Dispositional options which may be available to the intake officer are to cite, warn, and release, to place on informal probation, to refer to an agency outside the system, or to file a petition.[48] Cressey reports that the degree and direction in which juvenile offenders are diverted is influenced by the individual intake officer's conception of justice, his philosophy and theory of corrections, his knowledge of community resources, his relationships with other professional welfare workers, both within and without his department, his personal assumptions, attitudes, biases, and prejudices, the size of his caseload, the workload of his department and other subtle conditions.[49]

If the intake officer files a petition against a youth, the law may allow for a probation investigation to be conducted prior to the adjudication hearing. The court officer conducting this investigation may choose to divert the youth at this point. This investigation process is the last phase of juvenile justice system processing wherein diversion can occur without recourse to some form of adjudication.[50]

Probation departments frequently operate system-controlled diversion programs which fall into two areas. In the first area, there is an extension of the intake function, which usually involves *intake, crisis intervention* (1-3 sessions), and *long-term counseling*. Distinct treatment programs which offer specific services, usually counseling, are also operated under the auspices of the probation department.[51]

According to McDermott, diversion practices/programs operating outside the juvenile justice system can be classified[52] as paralegal programs, alternative legal structures, and independent nonlegal programs. *Paralegal programs* may be an offshoot or arm of the juvenile justice system and have varying degrees of control over clients. Referrals to this type program are usually controlled by legal agencies; consequently, an effort is made to maintain amiable relationships with the juvenile court and police. *Alternative legal structures* include those programs which transfer specific offense categories (e.g., status offenses) into alternative legal structures such as the welfare department. This type program may function as a parallel juvenile justice system immune from due process restrictions.

Independent nonlegal programs seek to maintain a nonlegal status and independence from the juvenile justice system.

Diversion programs operating outside the juvenile justice system may include, but are not necessarily limited to:

1. Nonresidential services
   a. Counseling and casework services
   b. Drug counseling
   c. Remedial educational programs
   d. Recreational programs
   e. Medical, legal and employment services

2. Residential services
   a. Emergency and temporary shelter care
   b. Specialized foster care
   c. Group home treatment programs
   d. Therapeutic communities for youths with drug problems

A significant number of diversion programs, both inside and outside the juvenile justice system, are controlled, either directly or indirectly, by the juvenile justice system. These programs practice the minimization of penetration approach to diversion;

therefore, participation in diversion programs at any sequential level short of an adjudication hearing is acceptable. As a result of this practice, many juveniles find themselves diverted from the courtroom to informal probation.

NEGATIVE CONSEQUENCES OF DIVERSION PRACTICES/PROGRAMS

In an exploratory study of diversion processes in juvenile justice, Cressey concluded:

1. Diversion programs established under the auspices of the juvenile justice system may distract attention from the criticism that led to their establishment in the first place.[53]

2. Juvenile justice system personnel operating diversion programs may simply revamp terminology and procedures without seriously altering what happens to the juvenile.[54]

3. Diversion programs may become a bureaucratic means of diverting attention from needed changes in the environment of youth and may serve to only perpetuate anachronistic institutions.[55]

McDermott (1976), in his national evaluation of juvenile diversion, stated that diversion programs may:[56]

1. Increase the number of youths who come into contact with the juvenile justice system.
2. Increase the budget and the staff of the system.
3. Result in more intensive handling of nondiverted youth.
4. Abandon traditional diversion processes (screening) in favor of diversion into the system.
5. Ignore juveniles' due process rights.
6. Increase the influence of legal authorities within private programs.
7. Create new legal entities.

Nejelski purported that diversion programs are dangerous to the extent that they may be only a halfway measure which takes pressure off the justice system to eliminate status offenses and, instead, create an equally coercive social control system with less visibility and accountability.[57]

EVALUATIONS OF DIVERSION PROGRAMS

Numerous evaluations of diversion programs have been accomplished. McDermott reported that studies of juvenile diversion have generally focused on client outcomes and/or systems impact and/or descriptions of processes/programs.

Client outcome studies have been primarily concerned with evaluations of program "success" as reflected by reduced recidivism rates. Key studies of this type are:[58]

Project Crossroads. Leon Leiber's study reported that diversion with referral was associated with lower rates of re-arrest than traditional modes of processing. Diversion accompanied by the provision of services also was viewed as more effective in terms of re-arrest rates than merely screening a youth out of the system. (See Leon Leiber, *Project Crossroads: A Final Report* to the *Manpower Administration,* Washington: National Committee for Children and Youth, U.S. Department of Labor, 1971.)

Sacramento 601-602 Diversion Project. Using re-arrest as a measure of recidivism, in a seven-month follow-up the researchers found that 30% of project youth were subsequently rearrested on 601 status offenses contrasted with 46% of the control group. Eighteen percent of project youth were rearrested on charges of criminal conduct compared to 31% of the control group. (See Warren Thornton, Edward Barrett and Lloyd Musolf, "The Sacramento County Probation Department 601 Diversion Project," Sacramento: Sacramento County Probation Department, 1972.)

Pre-Trial Intervention Diversion Project. Arnold Binder found that improving parent–child communication skills and teaching youth coping skills resulted in recidivism rates of 15% for the treated youths and 29% for the control group. Recidivism rates were based upon the results of a 6-month follow-up. Rates were operationalized as police arrests. (See Arnold Binder, "Pre-Trial Intervention and Diversion," Irvine Calif. University of Calif., 1974.) Suzanne Lincoln, "Juvenile Diversion Referral and Recidivism," in *Police*

Diversion of Juvenile Offenders, eds. Klein and Carter, 1974, (Englewood Cliffs: Prentice-Hall, 1975). Suzanne Lincoln studied a pilot diversion project which referred juveniles to community agencies for social services. The referred offenders were matched with nontreated juveniles of similar characteristics. With regard to the average seriousness of subsequent offenses, the referred and typical groups did not significantly differ. The two groups did differ on the average number of subsequent offenses. Juveniles in the referred groups showed a *higher* number of offenses. Lincoln concluded that referral tends to aggravate rather than to deter recidivism.

Criminal Recidivism and the New York City Project. Robert Fishman has recently completed an evaluation of rehabilitation and diversion services in New York City (adult and juvenile). The study primarily attempted to measure the result of recidivism as an outcome of such services. Police arrest rates were used as a measure of recidivism among 2,860 male clients. Fishman found that differences between projects did not affect recidivism rates. After one year of project contact he found that clients 18 or younger had higher recidivism rates and clients 21-39 [years old] had lower rates. He concluded that rehabilitation by New York City projects was a failure. (See Robert Fishman, "An Evaluation of the Effect on Criminal Recidivism of New York City Projects Providing Rehabilitation and Diversion Services" New York Criminal Justice Coordinating Council, 1975.)

An Impact Study of Two Diversion Programs. Delbert Elliot and Fletcher Blanchard have investigated the impact of two diversion programs on participating youths' attitudes, perceptions, and behavior. They described the objectives of both programs as being to increase perceived access to desirable social roles, to reduce the stigma associated with traditional processing within the juvenile justice system, to reduce feeling of alienation, and to reduce involvement in delinquent behavior. A casework approach was followed with intensive counseling for both the youngsters and their families. Other services were provided when this was deemed necessary. Comparison groups were obtained from youth placed on probation. Interviews were conducted with the four groups over a 12-month period and the researchers caution that a serious attrition problem should be noted when interpreting the results. Few differences were found between the diversion and probation samples, and only two of these were statistically significant. Self-esteem measures were lower for the diversion samples in both cities, and one diversion sample showed a greater perceived negative labeling. No differences were found in relation to impact on delinquency. (See Delbert S. Elliott and Fletcher Blanchard, "An Impact Study of Two Diversion Projects," paper presented at the American Psychological Assoc. Convention, Chicago, 1975.)

Systems impact studies attempt to measure structural and procedural changes in the juvenile justice system resulting from policies of diversion. Some systems impact studies are:[59]

> *National Evaluation of Youth Service Systems.* In 1974, Delbert Elliot examined seven youth service systems for the Office of Youth Development (HEW). It was assumed that a change in diversion could be measured across time as a percentage reduction in maintenance probabilities within the juvenile justice system. For each youth service system a set of baseline maintenance probabilities was established for two points in the juvenile justice system (police and probation intake). Although the research hoped to measure systems or institutional change, it was found that "most projects are making their entry into their communities via a direct service/diversion role and to date are not viewed primarily as agents pushing for institutional change." (See Delbert S. Elliott, "National Evaluation of Youth Service Systems," Boulder: The Office of Youth Development, Behavioral Research and Evaluation Corp., 1974.)
>
> *Alternate Routes Project.* Carter and Gilbert's evaluation of this project for the California Youth Authority indicated that in its counseling role the project was able to provide treatment more quickly than the juvenile justice system. The cost of processing was viewed as "considerably less expensive to the taxpayer than in the traditional juvenile justice system." The number of petitions filed was 6% for referred youths while 47% of regularly processed youths were petitioned. (See Robert Carter and John Gilbert, "Alternate Routes: An Evaluation," Sacramento: Department of California Youth Authority, 1973.)
>
> *The Sacramento 601-602 Diversion Project.* Utilizing short-term family crises therapy, the Sacramento project claims to have reduced petition filing from 21.5% (regular) to 2.2% (Project). (Thornton, et al., loc. cit.)
>
> *Los Angeles Police Diversion.* Malcolm Klein, attempted to account for variations among police department diversion rates. Klein and Sundeen were unable to account for great variation in terms of city size, population characteristics, demographic indices, police department size or structure, ratios of staff to clients or

arrestee characteristics. Sundeen attempted to account for the variations as resulting from degree of professionalism—with negative results. Klein concludes that diversion has minimal impact upon police operating procedures and/or department structure. He predicts diversion will have a short life, not outlasting current federal funding efforts. (See Malcolm Klein, "Police Processing of Juvenile Offenders: Toward the Development of System Rates," Los Angeles: L.A. County Criminal Justice Planning Board, 1970.)

Descriptions of processes/programs have been limited. A pilot study conducted by Cressey and McDermott for the National Assessment of Juvenile Corrections sought to explicitly address the problem of decision-making in diversion. Their general interests were exploratory and descriptive. Concentrating upon probation diversion, they concluded that the intake officer occupied the pivotal role in the diversion process. They described that role as dependent upon the subjective interpretation by the intake officer as to concepts of "justice," theories of corrections, and the "seriousness" of juvenile offenses and attitudes. The intake officer's knowledge of, and evaluation of, referral resources and his relationship with other workers inside and outside of the juvenile justice system were also seen as crucial for the quantity and quality of diversion. The informal relationship between diversion programs and intake units affected rates of diversion.[60]

In a review of nine evaluation studies of diversion projects, Gibbons and Blake concluded there was insufficient evidence in the nine studies to warrant one having much confidence in diversion arguments and contentions.[61]

A National Study of Youth Service Bureaus found that 64% of the directors of youth service bureaus included in the study thought that diversion was the primary objective of their organization. However, only 25% of the youths in their program were in immediate jeopardy of the juvenile justice system. This study concluded that it was impossible to prove that any significant number of youths had been diverted from the juvenile justice system by youth service bureaus.[62]

Based on data gathered from departmental interviews and over 3,000 case files in police departments, a project concerned with selected issues in the development of police programs for diverting youth from the juvenile justice system made the following findings:[63]

1. There are major differences in styles and levels of commitment in police diversion programs, and these relate differentially to types of offenders referred.
2. Evaluation components of the programs reviewed generally had little or no impact on the operations of the programs.
3. Referrals to community agencies have increased significantly over the past five years, but remain relatively low.
4. Referred youngsters, rather than being diverted from the justice system, are more commonly drawn from those ordinarily released without further action.
5. This pattern of referral as an alternative to release is strongly manifested in the variables of age, sex, prior record, and seriousness of instant offense.
6. Current police referral rates are very much a function of the infusion of outside Federal and State funds. In the absence of the continuation of such funds, our data imply that referral rates will recede toward their earlier, very low level.

Cressey reported that diversion is rather difficult to describe because of the multitude of diverse operative patterns and the paucity of systematic record-keeping by the agencies purporting to engage in diversion.[64] He also stated that the evaluation of diversion programs will be a time-consuming and expensive process without bright prospects of meaningful results, because of the limited quantity and lack of uniformity of information recorded by diversion program personnel.[65]

A DESCRIPTION OF FOUR DIVERSION PROGRAMS

Following is a description of the Sacramento County Diversion Program (Sacramento, California), the Mecklenburg County Youth Services Bureau (Charlotte, North Carolina), the Philadelphia Neighborhood Youth Resources Center (Philadelphia, Pennyslvania), and the Adolescent Diversion Project (Urbana-

Champaign, Illinois). All these diversion programs will be described in terms of their organization, funding source, location of office(s), goals related to diversion, degree to which diversion goals were achieved, primary referral source(s), target population, services, staff qualifications, type participation, type diversion practiced and impact of the program on the juvenile justice system.

Sacramento County Diversion Program

ORGANIZATION. This program was established as a diversion unit within and under the auspices of the Sacramento County Probation Department.

FUNDING SOURCE. Local government.

LOCATION OF OFFICE(S). The offices of this program were located within the Sacramento County Probation Department.

GOALS RELATED TO DIVERSION

> To reduce the number of cases going to court.
> To decrease the number of overnight detentions.
> To reduce the number of repeat offenses of program
> participants.

DEGREE TO WHICH DIVERSION GOALS WERE ACHIEVED

> Juvenile court petitions were reduced by 90%.
> Overnight detentions were reduced by 50%.
> The number of program participants involved in repeat
> offenses of any kind was reduced by 14%.

PRIMARY REFERRAL SOURCES. Police, schools and parents.

TARGET POPULATION. Status offenders referred to the juvenile court.

SERVICES.   Family counseling sessions (maximum of five sessions per family).
Referral to residential alternatives to detention (e.g., temporary shelter care).

STAFF QUALIFICATIONS.   Program staff possessed college degrees and had varying degrees of experience in a probation or social service agency.

TYPE PARTICIPATION.   Participation of clients was essentially voluntary; however, implicit and possibly explicit coercion were present.

TYPE DIVERSION PRACTICED.   Minimization of penetration.

IMPACT ON JUVENILE JUSTICE SYSTEM

Juvenile court petitions were reduced by 80%.
Overnight detentions were reduced by 50%.

ADDITIONAL INFORMATION.   The number of youths who engaged in criminal behavior after participation in the program was decreased by 25%.[66]
The cost of the diversion techniques used in this program was less than half the cost of procedures previously used by the probation department.[67]

Mecklenburg County Youth Services Bureau

ORGANIZATION.   This program was established as an agency of local government and is not controlled, either directly or indirectly, by any component of the juvenile justice system.

FUNDING SOURCE.   Local Government.

LOCATION OF OFFICES.   The offices of this program are located in a local government building on the same floor as the offices of the juvenile court.

GOALS RELATED TO DIVERSION.   To, during the 1976–77 fiscal year, divert a significant number of children from the juvenile court and/or correctional institutions by providing intensive counseling and casework services or intervention and referral services to a minimum of 300 children who are either involved or on the verge of becoming involved in the juvenile justice system because they are exhibiting behavior which has or is likely to bring them under the jurisdiction of the juvenile court as a status offender or delinquent.

To, by providing staff and technical assistance services to the Youth Services Action Board, assist the community and government to identify, implement, coordinate and monitor those services which are most needed by children who exhibit behavior which has or will likely bring them under the jurisdiction of the juvenile court as a status offender or delinquent.

DEGREE TO WHICH DIVERSION GOALS WERE ACHIEVED.[68,69]   Ninety percent or 314 of the 347 children served did not have a petition filed against them at the time of their referral to this program. Ninety percent or 284 of these 314 children had not become involved in the juvenile justice system as of June 30, 1977.

Ten percent or 33 of the 347 children had a petition filed against them at the time they were referred to this program. Eighty-two percent or 27 of these 33 children did not have additional petitions filed against them as of June 30, 1977.

Ninety-nine percent or 346 of the 347 children served had not been incarcerated in a juvenile correctional institution between the date of their referral to the YSB and June 30, 1977.

The Mecklenburg Youth Services Action Board, with staff and technical assistance services from the Youth Services Bureau staff, accomplished the following:

1.   Conducted an assessment of services most needed by Mecklenburg County children who exhibited behavior which had

or was likely to bring them under the jurisdiction of the juvenile court as a status offender or delinquent.

2. Persuaded local government officials to use federal, state and local funds to operate three group home treatment units and an emergency shelter care facility, to expand an alternative remedial education program, and to develop a specialized foster care program and specialized emergency foster care receiving homes.

3. Elicited support for a state law which eliminated status offenders from juvenile correctional institutions effective July 1, 1978 and disbursed block grants of funds to local units of government for the purpose of developing delinquency prevention and treatment services identified, delivered, and controlled at the local level.

4. Provided the community and government with data concerning both the number of children who were processed by the juvenile justice system and the nature of this processing.

PRIMARY REFERRAL SOURCES. Schools, juvenile court intake counselors, parents, juvenile court counselors, police, and youth service agencies.

TARGET POPULATION. Any child exhibiting behavior which had or could likely bring him/her under the jurisdiction of the juvenile court as a status offender or delinquent.

SERVICES. Intensive short-term (3½ months) counseling and casework services.

Intervention and referral services (intake, crisis counseling and referral to community services).

Provision of staff and technical assistance services to the Youth Services Action Board.

STAFF QUALIFICATIONS. Program staff possessed graduate degrees in a human service area and had experience working with youth.

TYPE PARTICIPATION. Voluntary participation.

TYPE DIVERSION PRACTICED.   True Diversion. In those cases which involved youths who had a legal status (i.e. post-petition, probation) at the time they were referred, this program technically served as an alternative to incarceration rather than as a diversion program. However, not all those youth (post-petition, probation) served were in immediate danger of incarceration at the time they were referred to this program.

IMPACT ₁ON THE JUVENILE JUSTICE SYSTEM.   During the period July 1, 1976, through June 30, 1977, when compared to the same period in 1973–74, the year in which this program first made its services available to the target group previously specified, there was:

1.   A 42% decrease in the number of petitions filed against youths alleging the commission of a status offense.

2.   A 35% reduction in the number of admissions to the detention center.

3.   A 43% decrease in the number of children incarcerated in state juvenile correctional institutions.

4.   A 43% reduction in the number of felony offenses and a 28% decrease in the number of misdemeanor offenses alleged in juvenile petitions filed against youth.

5.   A 35% decrease in the average number of active cases handled each month by juvenile court probation officers.

Heasley suggests that a number of factors influenced these reductions, not just this program.[70]

The Philadelphia Neighborhood Youth Resources Center[71]

ORGANIZATION.   This program was operated under the auspices of a private social service agency.

FUNDING SOURCE.   This program was supported by a federal grant.

LOCATION OF OFFICE(S).   The offices of this program were located in the high-crime inner-city area in which the target population resided.

GOALS RELATED TO DIVERSION.   To reduce the annual rate of referrals to the juvenile court by diverting youth away from the juvenile justice system into alternative programs.[71a]

DEGREE TO WHICH DIVERSION GOALS WERE ACHIEVED.   No data available.

PRIMARY REFERRAL SOURCE(S).   Schools, police, juvenile court, self-referral, staff referrals, and public and private agencies.

TARGET POPULATION.   Four thousand youths, 10 to 17 years of age, who resided in a 70-block urban ghetto.

SERVICES

>   Crises intervention.
>   Individual casework.
>   Group work involving counseling and educational assistance.
>   Referrals to cooperating agencies.
>   Legal representation.

STAFF QUALIFICATIONS.   This program was staffed by paraprofessionals who were familiar with the target area and its residents. The services of a lawyer, psychiatric social worker, and court liaison officer were purchased by this program.

TYPE PARTICIPATION.   Voluntary participation.

TYPE DIVERSION PRACTICED.   True diversion.

IMPACT ON JUVENILE JUSTICE SYSTEM.   No data available.

ADDITIONAL INFORMATION.   In order to facilitate referrals from the juvenile court, this program employed a court liaison officer, who was technically a probation officer. He supplied this program with the names and addresses of youth who had made contact with the system. The program staff then forwarded letters to these persons inviting them to use program services.

Urbana–Champaign Adolescent Diversion Project[72]

ORGANIZATION.   This program was operated under the auspices of the University of Illinois at Urbana–Champaign.

FUNDING.   This program was supported by a federal grant.

LOCATION OF OFFICE(S).   The offices of this program were located on the University campus.

GOALS RELATED TO DIVERSION.   To provide juveniles in the neighboring communities of Urbana and Champaign with an alternative to formal court proceedings by intervening at the point of police contact and offering counseling and social assistance.[72a]

DEGREE TO WHICH DIVERSION GOALS WERE ACHIEVED.   Reduced average number of police contacts and severity of police contacts per child during and after child's participation in program.

Reduced average number of court petitions and severity of court petitions filed per child during and after child's participation in program.

Improved school attendance of program participants.[73]

PRIMARY REFERRAL SOURCE.   Police.

TARGET POPULATION.   Juveniles who had committed misdemeanors and who had two or three prior contacts with the police.

SERVICES.   Counseling (behavioral contracting).

Social assistance (child advocacy—assisting child to gain access to needed services).

STAFF QUALIFICATIONS.   This program was staffed by college student volunteers.

TYPE PARTICIPATION. Voluntary participation of clients, with implicit coercion present at point when child and family were offered an opportunity to participate in program.

TYPE DIVERSION PRACTICED.   True diversion.

IMPACT ON JUVENILE JUSTICE SYSTEM.   No data available. Only 24 juveniles participated in this program during 1974–75.

RECOMMENDATIONS TO AMELIORATE DIVERSION PRACTICES/PROGRAMS

The increased support for the expansion of diversion practices/programs has generated a number of questions which have been answered in many different ways by those persons responsible for determining when and under what circumstances diversion is best utilized. These questions include, but are not necessarily limited to:

1. Should "true diversion" or "minimization of penetration" be the diversion practice employed?
2. Who should divert?
3. At what point should diversion occur?
4. Who should be diverted?
5. What criteria should be the basis for the decision to divert?
6. To what should youths be diverted?
7. Should diversion programs be controlled by the juvenile justice system?
8. What should be the goals of diversion practices/programs?
9. What measures should be utilized to evaluate diversion practices/programs?

Following are comments and recommendations promulgated in response to the foregoing questions.

Comment

The term true diversion refers to a discretionary act directed at forestalling adjudication which results in a termination of official intervention and/or referral of a youth to a program *outside* the juvenile justice system.[74] To wit, the youth is safely out of the realm of the system and, it is hoped, is immune from incurring the delinquent label.

Minimization of penetration refers to a process which results in further system intervention, usually by rerouting the youth to a diversion program within the juvenile justice system.[75]

In a national evaluation of diversion, McDermott found that minimization of penetration was clearly the predominant diversion practice being utilized. He reported that practitioners seemed to view the *intensity* and *degree* of processing to constitute the harm rather than the processing itself. In practice, diversion has come to mean keeping a child away from an adjudication hearing.[76]

A study by Cressey found that the further a youth proceeds into the juvenile justice system, the less the chances he/she will be diverted.[77]

A finding by the National Assessment of Juvenile Corrections was that research studies are consistently revealing that legal processing and sanctions do not have a deterrent effect on subsequent criminal behavior. In fact, the earlier youths are processed and the more stringent the sanction, the more likely it is that a youth will subsequently report or be processed for more serious criminal law violations.[78]

RECOMMENDATION.   The expenditure of federal, state, local and private funds for diversion programs should be limited to *only* those programs which practice "true diversion" as defined above.

Comment

During a single year, a community can expect approximately 8% of its youth, within the age jurisdiction of the juvenile court, to have some police contact. About 4% of a community's youth will be referred to the juvenile court. An estimated 2% of the youths referred to the juvenile court will have an adjudication hearing. The preceding information documents that police and probation intake officers are in an excellent position to practice diversion. In this regard, it is important to point out that police can divert youths *from* the system, but intake officers can only divert youths *out* of the system, or minimize their penetration into the system.

RECOMMENDATION. As the police level is the only point in the system at which youths can be diverted *from* the system, police should expand their diversion practices. Whenever possible, youths should be diverted at the police level.

Comment

The National Assessment of Juvenile Corrections reported that the majority of offenses of the youths referred to the juvenile court are offenses against property and status offenses. Status offenses comprise 40% of the referrals to the juvenile court.[79] Another NAJC finding was that the juvenile court possesses neither the resources nor the expertise to help youths who commit status offenses.[80]

Figlio, Sellin, & Wolfgang conducted a cohort study of 9,945 boys in Philadelphia.[81] Some important findings of this significant research effort were:

1. Between their 10th and 17th birthday, 3,475 (35%) members of the cohort had at least one police contact. These 3,475 youths committed 10,214 offenses during this period.[81a]

2. Of the 3,475 youths who had a police contact, 81% committed one (46%) or two (35%) offenses, then had no further police contact.[82] Only 6% or 627 members of this cohort were classified as chronic offenders. Persons who committed more than four offenses were classified as chronic offenders. Chronic offen-

ders committed more than one-half of the total offenses committed by the cohort.[83]

3. Seventy-two percent or 3,502 of the offenders experienced their first police contact between the ages of 12 and 16.[84]

4. Boys who committed a large number of offenses did so within a short time span. The mean age at the commission of the first offense on out to the 15th, for those boys who went that far, ranged from about 15 at the first offense to a little over age 16 at the 15th for all offense types taken together. It should also be noted that there were a large number of one-time offenders at ages 15–16.[85]

5. Beyond the third offense, desistence probabilities fall off. The greater the number of offenses, the more likely that serious offenses will be committed; therefore a reduction in recidivism should reduce the number of serious offenses.[86]

6. The likelihood of violent criminality increases with age, whereas the likelihood of property offense commission is irregular and both increases and decreases over age.[87]

7. Boys who received punitive treatment (fines, probation, institutionalization) were more likely to violate laws and commit more serious offenses with greater rapidity than those who had less constraining contact with the system.[88]

8. The juvenile justice system, at its best, has no effect on subsequent behavior of adolescent boys and, at its worst, has a deleterious effect on future behavior.[89]

Research studies also show that, whether caught by the police or not, about 80% of all juveniles commit one or two offenses and stop. To wit, most children become delinquent, but grow out of it. A few youths become chronic offenders.[90]

A finding in this cohort study was that the juvenile justice system isolates chronic offenders (those who commit four or more offenses) fairly well.[91] Nettler's review of studies of "hidden delinquency," lends support to this finding when he concludes:

> While some criminality is normal, persistent and grave violations of the law are the experience of a minority. This holds whether the measure is confessions or official statistics.[92]

RECOMMENDATION. 1. All youths who are referred to the police or juvenile court for committing a status offense should be diverted from or out of the juvenile justice system. 2. Excepting capital offenses, all youths who, according to police records, have committed less than three property and/or violent crimes, and who in the opinion of the police do not present an imminent threat to other persons or property, should be diverted from the juvenile justice system.

Comment

Bordua presented data for over 2,000 police agencies which showed that some police agencies released over 95% of the youth with whom they had contact, whereas, other police agencies sent nearly all apprehended youths to the juvenile court. He found that the level of delinquency reported by police to the juvenile courts was influenced by police department policies. Wilson's study which revealed differences in referral policies between two different police departments supported Bordua's findings.[93]

Police decision-making regarding juveniles is affected by many variables. Hohenstein and Sellin and Wolfgang have reported that the attitude of the victim frequently has much to do with the police decision to refer or not to refer a youth to the juvenile court. Other researchers have found that the demeanor a juvenile exhibits during his interaction with the police is an important variable which influences the dispositional decisions of police officers (Piliavin and Briar; Werthman and Piliavin).[94]

Although the decision-making criteria used by court intake workers are complex ones, it appears that they utilize the same types of information used by police in making dispositional decisions regarding youth.[95] Emerson's (1969) report on a juvenile court in a northern United States metropolitan area observed that intake officers arrived at decisions regarding juveniles in terms of judgments of moral character. That is to say, "bad kids" received harsh dispositions whereas those thought to be misguided youngsters were dealt with more leniently.[96] In their exploratory study of diversion processes in juvenile justice, Cressey reported that the degree and direction in which juvenile offenders are diverted is influenced by the individual intake officer's conception of justice, his philosophy and theory of corrections, his knowledge of community resources, his relationships with other professional welfare workers, both within and outside his department, his personal assumptions, attitudes, biases, and prejudices, the size of his caseload, the workload of his department, and other subtle conditions.[97] It would seem that the decision by police to divert or not to divert is influenced by variables similar to those considered by the intake officer.

RECOMMENDATION.   1.   The discretion used by police in making a determination about whether to divert or not divert a youth from the justice system should be reduced. This can be accomplished by police departments establishing policies which clearly specify those youths who should be referred to the juvenile justice system. The referrals to said system should be limited to: a. Those youths who commit capital offenses. b. Those youths who have committed less than three violent or property crimes and who, in the opinion of police, present an imminent threat to other persons or property. c. Those youths who, according to police records, have committed more than two violent or property crimes.

2.   As a general rule, police should not refer more than 2% of juveniles within the age jurisdiction of the juvenile court to said agency.

3.   The discretion utilized by probation intake officers in making a decision to divert or not divert a youth in the justice system should be decreased. This can be achieved if the juvenile court judge will indicate to the intake officer that youths who have an adjudicatory hearing should be limited to: a. Those youths who have committed capital offenses. b. Those youths who have committed less than three violent or property crimes and who, in the opinion of police, present an imminent threat to other persons or property. c. Those youths who have committed more than two violent or property crimes.

Comment

Most juvenile justice practitioners assert that many of those youths who exhibit behavior which could bring them under the jurisdiction of the juvenile court as a status offender or a delinquent must receive some type of treatment services to preclude more serious delinquent behavior. Consequently, many juvenile justice professionals and others argue that many youths cannot be diverted from the system because alternatives to the juvenile justice system are not available. They state that the services and concomitant authority provided by the juvenile court are needed to prevent future delinquency. Existing research, although beset with methodological problems, has not demonstrated that doing something (treatment services) is necessarily better than not doing anything.[98] This knowledge may make it easier for juvenile justice personnel and others to follow Shur's recommendation[98a] to "leave the kids alone whenever possible."

It seems clear that the juvenile justice system should significantly reduce the number of youths it processes; however, most youth service professionals would agree that youths deserve more than to simply avoid justice system processing. Many problem youths demonstrate a desperate need for emergency and temporary shelter care services, intensive counseling and casework services, alternative remedial educational services, specialized foster care services, group home treatment, and legal, medical, and employment services. The aforesaid services should be the services to which many youths are referred who are diverted from the juvenile justice system. In a number of cases, it will be necessary for the police and probation intake officers to effect these referrals. Consequently, these officials must assume more responsibility for linking youths with needed services.

RECOMMENDATION.   1.   Police and probation intake officers should assist their communities to identify, develop, and deliver those diversion services for which youths diverted from the juvenile justice system demonstrate the greatest need.
    2.   Police and probation intake officers should meet with the

parents or guardians of those youths diverted from the system as many times as are required to assure that these parents utilize diversion services. Parental participation in diversion programs should augment the chances that constructive actions will be taken to remediate the behavior of those youths diverted. In those cases where a diverted youth's parents are unable or unwilling to provide the youth with the supervision and discipline necessary to effect an improvement in the youth's behavior, it may be appropriate for the police or intake officer to take actions to accomplish an out of home placement for the youth.

Comment

In an exploratory study of diversion processes in juvenile justice, Cressey concluded:

1. Diversion programs established under the auspices of the juvenile justice system may distract attention from the criticism that led to their establishment in the first place.[99]

2. Juvenile justice system personnel operating diversion programs may simply revamp terminology and procedures without seriously altering what happens to the juvenile.[100]

3. Diversion programs may become a bureaucratic means of diverting attention from needed changes in the environment of youth and may serve to only perpetuate anachronistic institutions.[101]

In a national evaluation of juvenile diversion, McDermott found that diversion programs may:[102]

1. Increase the number of youths who come into contact with the juvenile justice system.

2. Increase the budget and the staff of the system.

3. Result in more intensive handling of nondiverted youths.

4. Abandon traditional diversion processes (screening) in favor of diversion into the system.

5. Ignore juveniles' due process rights.

6. Increase the influence of legal authorities within private programs.

7. Create new legal entities.

There is convincing evidence that millions of taxpayer dollars are being expended for diversion programs which actually widen the net of the juvenile justice system. This is particularly true of diversion programs operated by the justice system.

RECOMMENDATION. 1. Diversion programs should *not* be controlled, either directly or indirectly, by the juvenile justice system, should be noncoercive, and should seek to function as advocates for youth they serve.
2. Serious consideraton should be given to operating "private" diversion programs as they are more flexible in the deployment of staff, elicit more community support, allow for greater innovation, and can modify or eliminate ineffective programs easier than public programs.

Comment

Research findings by Figlio et al.[103] indicate that involving a youth in the juvenile justice system increases the likelihood that youth will commit more frequent and serious criminal law violations.

Although some researchers report that research evidence supporting the theory that labeling a child as delinquent causes that child to engage in further delinquency is skimpy at best and contradictory at worst, it is clear that many youth who penetrate the justice system perceive themselves as being labeled as criminals. In a national study of juvenile correction programs, Vinter[104] found that about 50% of all youth committed to juvenile corrections programs perceived themselves as being labeled as criminal.

The differential association delinquency causation theory states that youths engage in delinquent behavior because they experience an overabundance of interactions, associations, and reinforcements with behavior patterns favorable to delinquency. Consequently, potential delinquents should not be cast into interaction with more experienced ones. The importance of the peer group in shaping and controlling behavior has been stressed by both sociocultural and psychological theorists. Three pilot studies have identified some of the behavioral processes associated with shaping and controlling behavior within a peer group of delinquent adolescents. A major finding of these studies was that, within an institutional setting, the delinquent peer group provides massive schedules of positive reinforcement for deviant behavior and punishment for socially conforming behavior. This finding indicates that delinquent adolescents might be expected to provide an excellent opportunity for maintaining existing deviant behavior, and for the novice an opportunity to acquire new sets of deviant behavior.[105]

RECOMMENDATION. All diversion programs should establish measurable goals and objectives. The major goal of diversion programs should be to significantly reduce the number of youths who become involved in the juvenile justice system. To wit, diversion programs should serve as substitutes for rather than supplements to the justice system.

Comment

Gibbons and Blake recommend that evaluations of diversion programs should include components which address the following questions:[106]

1. *Effectiveness Evaluation*
    a. Was the program in fact directed at the population for which it was intended?
    b. Did the program experience difficulty gaining access to target clients?
    c. Were there obstacles to initiating the program with target clients?
2. *Efficiency Evaluation*
    a. What was the frequency and quality of service delivery?
    b. To what degree were the processes, activities, and strategies of intervention actually implemented?
3. *Impact Evaluation*

What were the intended ends or consequences of intervention? To wit, did intervention result in reduced recidivism, improve school attendance, or effect attitudinal changes, etc.?

4. *Juvenile Justice Impact*

a. Did the program effect an increase in community tolerance of youthful deviance?

b. Did the program alter police and probation department referral practices?

c. Did the program cause a decrease in the number of children who became involved in the juvenile justice system?

A national study of youth service bureaus concluded that a significant increase or decrease in arrests, court petitions, etc., cannot be attributed to a particular community program. Rather, the entire youth service system or nonsystem has to be considered in regard to responsibility and accountability. To determine the degree and reason for diversion from the juvenile justice system, one must consider the system *from* which youths are being diverted before and after creation of diversion programs, as well as the system or nonsystem to which youths have been or could have been diverted.[107]

RECOMMENDATION.   Diversion programs should be evaluated in terms of the progress which they make toward achieving their measurable goals and objectives.

It is believed the foregoing recommendations are in the interests of youths, the juvenile justice system, and taxpayers. They should be given serious consideration by those responsible for implementing diversion practices/programs.

Deinstitutionalization: A Response to Overincarceration

Institutionalization: Its Extent and Characteristics
    Size of Correctional Facilities
        Private Institutions
        Other Characteristics
        Rapid Turnover and Multiple Transactions
    Institutionalization Rates: Gross Variations
    Cost of Institutionalization
Adverse Effects of Institutionalization
    Damages of Total Institutions
    Custodial Institution: A Totalitarian Regime
People-Changing Technologies: Lack of Standards
    Custodial Versus Treatment Institutions: Differential Impact
A Movement Toward Deinstitutionalization and Community-Based Alternatives
    Deinstitutionalization: Extent and Cost
    Foster Homes: Another Alternative
Experiments in Deinstitutionalization
    Highfields Experiment
    Silverlake Experiment
    Provo Experiment
    A Radical Strategy: Closing of Training Schools
        Recidivism
    Community Treatment Project (CTP)
        Results
        Second Phase of Experiment (1969-1974)
Youth Service Bureaus (YSB)
Summary and Conclusions

Chapter 5

DEINSTITUTIONALIZATION

A Response to Overincarceration

Deincarceration or deinstitutionalization can be defined as the removal from secure detention and correctional institutions of those youths who can be handled or treated better in an alternative setting without any risk to the safety of society. Alternatives to incarceration may include *(1)* probation, *(2)* community-based residential and nonresidential programs, and *(3)* foster care. Before a case is made for deinstitutionalization, the extent and effects of incarceration will be examined.

INSTITUTIONALIZATION: ITS EXTENT AND CHARACTERISTICS

Large-scale incarceration of juveniles has already been discussed in the first two chapters. However, a few additional facts will be mentioned here to place institutionalization of children in a proper perspective.

During 1971, approximately 616,766 juveniles and nonjuveniles were processed by public juvenile detention and correctional facilities (not counting the admissions in jails and private institutions). During 1973, admissions to these same institutions were decreased to 600,601 (a 3% reduction). During this same period, admissions and departures at halfway houses and group homes increased by approximately 120%.[1] These figures would seem to indicate that a process of deinstitutionalization is occuring in the United States. However, this assumption seems somewhat premature based on the mid-year census for the years 1974 and 1975 (see Tables 5.1 and 5.2). Although it is encouraging to find an increase of 23% in halfway houses and group homes, it is distressing to learn that a 5–6% increase in population of all other short- and long-term institutions has also occurred. Apparently, as new halfway houses and group homes open, juvenile authorities use them as additional housing for incarceration. Thus, community-based residential centers were used as a supplement rather than a substitute for juvenile security institutions. At least this was the situation in 1975. Post-1975 statistics in regard to deinstitutionalization in favor of community-based programs are not available at this writing. It is hoped that post-1975 data will reveal that there has been a significant shift away from security institutions to residential facilities in the community.

Size of Correctional Facilities

In 1971, there were 12 training schools in the United States with a capacity to hold 500 or more youths. Most juvenile justice experts agree that large institutions are not compatible with the modern concept of treatment of delinquents. Fortunately for youths and taxpayers, only nine of these institutions were in operation in 1973.[2] It is hoped that all large juvenile correctional institutions will be phased out soon. As long as there are massive institutions, there is a tendency on the part of court and correctional personnel to fully utilize these "warehouses" for youths.

Table 5.1.   Selected Characteristics of Public Juvenile Detention and Correctional Facilities--United States, 1974 and 1975.

Characteristic	1974	1975	% Change
Facilities			
All facilities	829	874	+5
Short-term	371	387	+4
Detention centers	331	347	+5
Shelters	21	23	+10
Reception or diagnostic centers	19	17	-11
Long-term	458	487	+6
Training schools	185	189	+2
Ranches, forestry camps, and farms	107	103	-4
Halfway houses and group homes	166	195	+17
Juveniles held in			
All facilities	44,922	46,980	+5
Short-term	12,566	12,725	+1
Detention centers	11,010	11,089	+1
Shelters	180	200	+11
Reception or diagnostic centers	1,376	1,436	+4
Long-term	32,356	34,255	+6
Training schools	25,397	26,748	+5
Ranches, forestry camps, and farms	5,232	5,385	+3
Halfway houses and group homes	1,727	2,122	+23
Sex of juveniles held			
Both sexes	44,922	46,980	+5
Male	34,783	37,926	+9
Female	10,139	9,054	-11
Detention status of juveniles held			
All juveniles	44,922	46,980	+5
Adjudicated delinquents	31,270	34,107	+9
Persons in need of supervision (PINS)	4,644	4,494	-3
Held pending court disposition	7,373	7,011	-5
Awaiting transfer to another jurisdiction	458	392	-14
Voluntary admission	679	516	-24
Dependent and neglected	498	460	-9
Payroll and nonpayroll staff			
Total	46,276	52,534	+14
Full-time	39,391	41,156	+4
Part-time	6,885	11,378	+65
Average population	46,753	48,794	+4
Per capita operating expenditures	10,354	11,471	+11

Source: U.S. Department of Justice, Children in Custody, 1975, Law
Enforcement Assistance Administration, Washington, D.C., 1977.

Table 5.2. Selected Characteristics of Private Juvenile Detention and Correctional Facilities--United States, 1974 and 1975.

Characteristic	1974	1975	% Change
Facilities			
All facilities	1,337	1,277	-4
Short-term	76	66	-13
Long-term	1,261	1,211	-4
Training schools	61	65	+7
Ranches, forestry camps, and farms	395	295	-25
Halfway houses and group homes	805	851	+6
Juveniles held in			
All facilities	31,749	27,290	-14
Short-term	797	830	+4
Long-term	30,952	26,460	-15
Training schools	4,078	3,660	-10
Ranches, forestry camps, and farms	16,955	13,094	-23
Halfway houses and group homes	9,919	9,706	-2
Sex of juveniles held			
Both sexes	31,749	27,290	-14
Male	22,104	19,152	-13
Female	9,645	8,138	-16
Detention status of juveniles held			
All juveniles	31,749	27,290	-14
Adjucicated delinquent	9,874	9,809	-1
Persons in need of supervision (PINS)	4,969	4,316	-13
Held pending court disposition or awaiting transfer to another jurisdiction	544	529	-3
Voluntary admission	7,635	5,879	-23
Dependent and neglected	7,104	4,844	-32
Other[a]	1,623	1,913	+18
Payroll and nonpayroll staff			
Total	28,612	27,651	-3
Average population	31,384	26,735	-15
Per capita operating expenditures	8,543	9,518	+11

[a]Represents emotionally disturbed or mentally retarded juveniles awaiting transfer for specialized treatment.

Source: U.S. Department of Justice, Children in Custody, 1975. Washington, D.C.: U.S. Government Printing Office, 1977.

The clear relation (.59) between the sizes of average daily populations in all of these facilities and the sizes of average populations per facility suggests that the greater the state's total numbers handled through such programs, the more likely they are to be assigned to larger rather than to smaller facilities.[3]

Training schools come in all sizes ranging from a small facility which may hold 25 residents to a large institution where 500 or more youths can be confined. The median size juvenile correctional institutions can hold about 160 residents. Community-based residential centers are smaller. The 1973 census revealed that 89% of shelters and 85% of halfway houses for youths were designed for fewer than 25 residents. Seventy-three percent of detention centers had a design capacity for fewer than 50 residents.[4] State-operated juvenile facilities tended to have larger design capacities than institutions run by local units of government.

PRIVATE INSTITUTIONS.   As is evident from Tables 5.1 and 5.2, there are more private institutions than public institutions, but private institutions hold smaller numbers of youths. Public institutions hold 63% of the total number of juveniles institutionalized compared to 36% held by private institutions. Private institutions are mostly for long-term care (or confinement), with a high percentage of youths in such facilities as ranches, forestry camps, and farms. Proportionately, private institutions hold more girls and PINS. A large number of youths, on whose behalf voluntary admission is sought, prefer to be sent to private rather than public institutions. Although private facilities are relatively less expensive than public institutions, they are decreasing in number and population.

Other Characteristics

About one-half of juvenile detention and correctional facilities admitted both males and females at the time of the 1973 census. The number of coeducational institutions has shown a steady increase. Juveniles under the jurisdiction of the state authorities are far more likely to be segregated on the basis of sex than those in locally administered facilities. Seventy-seven percent of juveniles in state facilities, compared with 26% in local institutions, were confined in facilities limited to one sex in 1973.[5]

The 1973 census shows that females made up 31% of all juveniles held in detention centers; 37% in shelters; 21% in reception or diagnostic centers; 23% in training schools; 6% at ranches, forestry camps, and farms; and 27% in halfway houses and group homes.[6] Whereas the average age of male residents held in these facilities was 15.2 years, the age of female residents was 14.9 years. In 1973, residents of training schools were confined, on the average, for the longest period (in excess of 7 months), whereas youths placed in detention centers were held the shortest periods (less than 2 weeks).[7] Training school authorities, who cannot control the number of youth committed to these institutions by the court prefer to keep their wards a minimum of six to seven months to organize a "suitable" program for them. Youths may or may not consider training school helpful.

Rapid Turnover and Multiple Transactions

Regardless of whether institutional programs are helpful or harmful to youths, the institutional population has to experience a number of transactions. As a youth is moved from one institution to another, he or she has to make a new adjustment. Relationships developed in the context of rapid turnover in institutions are transient in nature.

> The large annual volume of admissions and departures, many times larger than the average daily population residing in public juvenile detention and correctional facilities, reflected the rapid turnover characteristic of the nation's juvenile justice system. It also reflected the multiple transactions involved in processing those individuals ultimately committed to a long-term facility, particularly to training schools or to ranches, forestry camps, and farms. The transactions for such persons might show initial intake at a detention center, referral to a reception or diagnostic center for evaluation, assignment to the relevant long-term facility, and, not infrequently, recommitment for a new offense or readmission for failure in an aftercare or parole program.[8]

Institutionalization Rates: Gross Variations

Heavy reliance on incarceration is nationwide, yet not all states are equally contributing to incarceration. In fact, there is great variability in incarceration rates. Judging from 1974 rates of average daily institutional population, Wyoming incarcerated 41.3 juveniles per 100,000 of the total state population, whereas New York incarcerated only 2.1 juveniles per 100,000 of its state population. Wyoming's rate (the highest) was 20 times the rate of New York (the lowest), the mean rate being 17.8. Reasons for interstate variability in incarceration rates have not been adequately investigated, but there is some indication that less wealthy, more rural, and less industrialized states appear to have a greater reliance on incarceration.[9]

It is worth noting that the per capita rate of institutionalization is negatively correlated with states' percentages of urban population (−.38), per capita income (−.31), industrialization (−.44), and Walker's index of general state innovativeness (−.59). Thus, wealthier, more urbanized and industrialized states, which are frequently among the first to depart from traditional policy alternatives, appear less likely to rely heavily on the use of juvenile institutions and camps. Furthermore, we can assert that the greater reliance on these facilities in the less wealthy, more rural, and less industrialized states is *not* due to any greater prevalence of juvenile crime. In fact, the correlation between institutionalization and the overall crime rate is −.10 and its correlation with the property crime rate is −.08.[10]

This is an outstanding finding. If the rate of incarceration bears no correlation to the rate of crime, states with a relatively lower rate of incarceration are achieving the same results as those states which warehouse large numbers of youth. What is the justification for this heavy reliance on detention centers and correctional institutions? Even if the mean rate of incarceration (17.8) is accepted as a satisfactory dividing point, 22 states are incarcerating at a higher rate. Incarcerating children (and adults too) is an ideology devoid of any scientific support. It is more an attitude or practice which some find very difficult to alter. States which are overincarcerating youths are not only failing to protect society, but, by this action, may be increasing the likelihood that many of these youths will commit more serious delinquency acts. Taxpayers are adversely affected by overincarceration because their money is being spent wastefully on keeping youths in institutions when many of these could be handled more effectively and at less expense outside institutions.

Cost of Institutionalization

In 1975, states spent close to $600 million on public juvenile detention and correctional facilities alone, and private facilities cost another $274 million (See Tables 5.1 and 5.2). The average cost per offender year in public facilities has been steadily increasing from $7,002 in 1971 to $9,577 in 1973 and $11,471 in 1975.[11] States varied greatly in what they spent annually on institutionalized youth. Three states spent an average amount between $3,500 to $4,999; eleven states incurred an average cost between $5,000 and $7,999; average cost per offender in the year 1974 for ten states ranged from $14,000 to $18,999; and four states spent above $19,000.[12] This disparity in expenditures evokes several questions: If the highest expenditure states needed over $19,000 to maintain their juveniles in institutions, what kind of institutional services were offered by states with the lowest expenditures? Furthermore, what kind of community-based treatment services could be offered for juveniles incarcerated in institutions at an annual cost to state taxpayers of over $20,000 per youth?

ADVERSE EFFECTS OF INSTITUTIONALIZATION

Damages of Total Institutions[13]

In order to learn how residential institutions affected their inmates, Erving Goffman spent time with inmates of a large hospital. Goffman classifies custodial institutions as "total institutions." According to Goffman, a total institution is a place of residence and work where a large number of like-situated individuals, cut off from society outside for an appreciable period of time, lead an enclosed, formally administered way of life.[14] Custodial institutions, especially security institutions, separate their wards from the society outside. These inmates become accustomed to living with other residents of the institution, and become disinclined to adjust to family living. Total institutions generally fail to provide a natural setting for training its residents for normal living outside the institution. In fact, these institutions often "untrain" their residents to manage certain features of their daily life on the outside.[15] Total institutions often do not motivate inmates to work and often do not provide a proper setting for inmates to learn needed skills.

Total institutions impair self-esteem of inmates who have to go through a series of institutional procedures which are humiliating. For example, frequently boys will be subjected to rectal examinations and girls are required to submit to pelvic examinations. Entrants are undressed, disinfected, photographed, and fingerprinted.[16] They are dispossessed of their meager personal belongings (e.g., clothes, pens, watches, jewelry, cosmetics, girdles, and in some cases even combs and shaving sets). Their personal items are stored away, and they are issued institutional clothes. There are dress codes and regulations on hair length. Adolescents dislike these codes and perceive them as personal defacement.[17] These youths realize they are no longer children of their families, but rather inmates in an impersonal world who have been dispossessed of their previous roles.

Inmates are continually subjected to a process of *mortification of self*. They sleep collectively in barracks and use toilets without doors. They are searched by guards and sexually assaulted by their own peers. They must adjust to all of these privations and deprivations. Inmates seek various forms of adjustment. Some become pro-staff, others reject their rejectors, rather than themselves. Some make the institution their home (colonization), whereas others seek stable sexual ties, and make friends (fraternalization). Some tend to withdraw from all of this and develop signs of acute depersonalization and prison psychosis.[18]

Custodial Institution: A Totalitarian Regime

Sykes' study of a maximum security prison (1958)[19] includes a number of findings relevant to security institutions for juveniles. The security institution represents a social system of total social control.

> The detailed regulations extending into every area of the individual's life, the constant surveillance, the concentration of power into the hands of a ruling few, the wide gulf between the rulers and the ruled—all are elements of what we usually call a totalitarian regime.[20]

Staff members in these institutions receive numerous orders from their supervisors; and in time, they issue many orders to the inmates. However, inmates frequently do not view these orders as legitimate and do not feel compelled to obey them.

Life in security institutions is extremely depriving and frustrating to the inmates. This deprivation is exemplified by the inmates' loss of goods and services. The loss of material possessions in the western world is a very ego-deflating experience, particularly in the case of youths. In one-sex institutions, youths have little or no opportunity to interact with peers of the opposite sex. This *denial of heterosexual interaction* can be very depriving for sexually active adolescents. It is well known that inmates in closed institutions switch to homosexuality either voluntarily or involuntarily. There is also a *deprivation of security*. Some peaceful inmates become easy victims at the hands of more violent ones. One of the most difficult things for a prisoner is to live with other prisoners. There is a *deprivation of autonomy*. Inmates are subjected to a vast body of regulations, hampering their spirit of self-determination.[21]

Sykes contends that security institutions are entrusted with the task of changing criminals, but staff members of these institutions are confused and ambivalent about the goals of these institutions, and are also uncertain about the means to achieve the task of changing people.[22] To many staff members in custodial institutions, rehabilitation concepts are irrelevant, theoretical, and distant.[23] Staff members are poorly trained, low paid, and disenchanted with their working conditions.

PEOPLE-CHANGING TECHNOLOGIES: LACK OF STANDARDS

There is little standardization in people-changing technologies. Each administrator seems to have his or her favorite philosophy, fully convinced of its merit. Unfortunately, many of these philosophies have never been subjected to proper empirical testing and evaluation.

The ends sought in people-changing have an abstract quality; there is difficulty not only in proving one technique more successful than another, but also in assessing performance, even given a particular technology. At present, widely different technologies compete in virtually all people-changing organizations. Further, there is much borrowing among types: For example, military models are often used in correctional organizations, as are various technologies prevalent in case-work agencies and mental hospitals.[24]

In an empirical study, Street, Winter, and Perrow found that juvenile custodial institutions affected inmates much more adversely than reeducation and treatment institutions.

Custodial Versus Treatment Institutions: Differential Impact

As institutions differ in size, goals, and philosophy of treatment, so do they differ in their impact on inmates. Street et al. thought that the belief system (delinquents are treatable or untreatable) and the institutional goals (custodial versus treatment) are the prime movers in the impact of treatment. "As the goals of organizations change under the impact of treatment concepts, staff attitudes, inmate orientations and inmate leadership structures alter."[25] Street et al. present sets of beliefs which fall into three categories.

1. *Authority and Obedience*. Inmates must learn to obey the authorities. The experience of incarceration and deprivation will make them change their deviant behavior.

2. *Learning and Socialization*. Delinquents who have not learned good habits for lack of proper schooling can learn good habits if they are involved in a learning process—for example, academic and vocational programs. Those who were not well nurtured in a disorganized family should be socialized in the secure and supportive environment of a cottage parent system.

3. *Therapy*. On account of deep-seated deviance, rehabilitation should take place through extensive changes in character and personality. The methods employed are individual, group, and milieu therapies.

INSTITUTIONAL MODELS.   To parallel these belief systems, the researchers selected three organizational models, ranged along the custody-treatment continuum. Six institutions (three large and public, three small and private) corresponded to the following models, with two institutions in each category:

1. *Obedience/Conformity Model*. The two custodial institutions used coercive methods.

2. ⹁ *Reeducation/Development Model*. The two institutions sent children to community schools for academic and vocational training during the day.

3. *Treatment Model*. The two therapy-oriented institutions used individual and group therapies to reconstitute the individuals. The three sets of institutions were selected by researchers to maximize differences in the goals and strategies used to change inmates.[26] A comparative view of the characteristics of the three institutional categories is given in Table 5.3.

Table 5.3. Institutions and Their Properties: A Comparative View

Dimension	Obedience/conformity Institutions	Reeducation/Development Institutions	Treatment Institutions
Assumptions	Inmates would learn to conform out of fear of consequences	Inmates possess resources that could be drawn upon and developed	Deviance could be corrected only by a thoroughgoing reorientation
Strategy to change people	Demanded compliance and submission	Sought moderate changes through training for a gainful career	Sought broad changes, altered personalities, improved interpersonal relations
Staff attitudes	Staff used coercive methods; staff pessimistic of inmate change	Used reeducation methods; staff optimistic of inmate change	Used more differentiated and voluntaristic methods; staff optimistic of inmate change
Authority	Cottage staff had most authority	Balanced distribution authority	Clinicians had most authority
Decision making	Decisions made about inmates without any personal cooperation	Some personal consideration	Decisions made about inmates with their consent and personal input
Volunteers	Not accepted	Welcomed	Welcomed
STAFF PERSPECTIVE Relationship	Staff members perceived staff-inmate understanding as difficult	Staff members perceived staff-inmate understanding as helpful	Staff members firmly believed in mutual understanding as a key factor in treatment
Discipline	Discipline emphasized	Balance between discipline and permissiveness	Permissiveness emphasized
INMATES' PERSPECTIVE	Inmates perceived the institution and staff negatively	Inmates' perceptions positive	Inmates perceived the institution and staff positively
Inmate Organization	Because of high deprivations, inmates tended to organize themselves cohesively to procure legitimate and illegitimate items of value	Group formation tended to be more after the pattern of treatment institutions	Inmates tended to organize more voluntarily around friendship patterns; inmate friendships were not anti-staff and the groups tended to be pro-staff
Inmate Leadership	Inmate leadership highly involved in illicit and secret activities; inmate leaders tended to gather power by controlling illicit rewards; leaders presented solidary opposition to staff	Leaders were a good influence for the inmates; they were not anti-staff in any way	Inmate leadership was positive and constructive in its outlook; there was no need for the leaders to gather power as there was no quest for illicit rewards; leaders were prepared to act along with staff

The most important finding by this comparison is that the institutions differ in the damaging effects of total institutionalization. As institutions become less depriving, more democratic, and more treatment oriented, inmate groups become less opposed to staff, more favorable to the staff, and more receptive to treatment technologies. A noteworthy observation is that *inmate background attributes did not account for this variation.*[27] *The variations in impact on inmates are the result of institutional goals and staff attitudes toward the control and treatment of their wards.* Street et al. also point to the self-fulfilling prophecies of the respective staffs. For example, the staff of the obedience/conformity institutions perceived their inmates negatively and tried to suppress them; the inmates reacted disruptively. In contrast, the staffs at treatment institutions were not overly concerned about inmates' threats to institutional stability; they found that such threats usually did not come to fruition.[28] So staff attitudes are important; output depends on input.

A MOVEMENT TOWARD DEINSTITUTIONALIZATION AND COMMUNITY-BASED ALTERNATIVES

Traditional alternatives to incarceration have included probation, parole, and halfway houses. These types of alternatives have been in existence for a long time, but a greater emphasis has been placed on them during the 1970s. A major impetus for the use of alternatives to incarceration came from the President's Commission on Law Enforcement and the Administration of Justice in 1967.

The Commission's second objective—the development of a far broader range of alternatives for dealing with offenders—is based on the belief that, while there are some who must be completely segregated from society, there are many instances in which segregation does more harm than good.

. . . every community (should) consider establishing a Youth Service Bureau, a community-based center . . .

To make community-based treatment possible for both adults and juveniles, the Commission recommends the development of an entirely new kind of correctional institution: located close to population centers.[29]

A few years later, the National Advisory Commission on Criminal Justice Standards and Goals (1973) set a goal for states to "refrain from building any more State institutions for juveniles." The Commission further desired that ". . . states should phase out present institutions over a five-year period."[30] A year later, Congress passed the Juvenile Justice and Delinquency Prevention Act of 1974 which gave a prominent place to community-based corrections. Sec. 223(H) "discourages the use of secure incarceration" and requires an "increased use of nonsecure community-based facilities as a percentage of total commitments to juvenile facilities."[31]

Deinstitutionalization: Extent and Cost

Despite the recommendation of various commissions concerning community-based corrections, security facilities still continue to be the dominant choice for confinement. Like the rate of incarceration in security facilities, the rate of admissions to community programs has varied greatly. According to a 1974 survey, some states moved very few juveniles to community-based residential centers and many of these states used these centers as supplements rather than as substitutes for traditional security institutions. The states with a better-educated citizenry seemed to take a more favorable view of community services. Community-based programs were not receiving a significant portion of states' budget allocations for juvenile corrections. Some community programs were operated by the state, others were only funded by the state, but operated by other agencies, mostly private. The latter arrangement was less expensive. The survey indicated that deinstitutionalization had occurred to the greatest extent in those states that relied heavily on purchase-of-service or other vendor arrangement. This 1974 survey also found community-based programs to be less expensive[32] than institutions, but concluded that a substantial proportion of the population of juvenile institutions must be transferred to community programs to effect budgetary savings.

The potential economies of deinstitutionalization cannot be gained when it is introduced at very modest levels, when community programs expand the total size of state correctional services and costly institutional facilities must also be maintained, or when it is approached primarily through the relatively more expensive state-run programs. The combination of all of these factors would actually raise both the states' overall expenditures and the rates of juvenile correctional programming.[33]

To effect a reasonable saving in expenditures, states may have to make a bold decision to phase out half of their security institutions. The 1974 Report prepared by the National Assessment of Juvenile Corrections estimated that if 50% of the institutional population was deinstitutionalized, each state could have saved an average of $1,232,100 after paying for their community-based programs.[34] Four states had actually reached or exceeded this level of 50% deinstitutionalization by 1974.

Foster Homes: Another Alternative

Vinter et al. discovered that some states used foster home placement of juvenile offenders at surprisingly high levels. Typically, one or two young offenders were placed in a single-family home for varying periods of time. On an average day in 1974, as many as 7,100 delinquents were assigned to foster homes in all states—a total considerably larger than the 5,663 reportedly assigned to community-based facilities. States reported an expense of about $9 million for foster care, as compared to $30 million spent on other community-based programs. Foster home placement seems to be the least costly residential service, even with the expenditure of additional funds to improve the quality of foster homes. The development of high-quality specialized foster care has excellent potential for extending community corrections. In 1974, states assigned five times as many youths to institutions as to community-based programs and four times as many as were placed in foster homes.

EXPERIMENTS IN DEINSTITUTIONALIZATION

Highfields Experiment

One of the earliest experiments in deinstitutionalization was the Highfields.[35] One of the purposes of this project was to determine if a new type of treatment center could be introduced which had none of the institutional patterns of a reformatory. Of the several experiments in residential milieu therapy, the Highfields experiment stands out as a classic. Boys adjudicated by the courts were randomly distributed between Highfields (the experimental group) and a reformatory (the control group). The Highfields boys worked in the community during the day and were bused back to the center in the evening. The Highfields was a small residential center that could accommodate 20 boys at a time. The usual stay at the center was about three months. The center was operated administratively by two or three people.

Group sessions, supervised by a trained therapist, were held five evenings a week. During their group meetings, the participants used a method known as "guided group interaction." Guided group interaction focuses on here-and-now interpersonal interactions, rather than on internal processes. Intense discussion revolves around the current problems and experiences of the group members.

The research addressed itself to measuring the effect of the Highfields experiment on (1) recidivism, (2) expressed attitudes toward families and law and order, and (3) the basic personality structure. The boys released through Highfields showed a lower rate of recidivism than those given reformatory releases. However, the Highfields treatment did not bring about any significant change in their attitudes or in their personality characteristics. (It should be noted that black boys showed greater success with the experiment than white boys.) In sum, residential centers seem to have a different impact on different types of offenders.

The Highfields study was followed by two similar studies in New Jersey, known as the Essexfields and Collegefields.

Silverlake Experiment

Silverlake is another experiment in deinstitutionalizaton.[36] A primary purpose of this experiment was to measure the impact of a community-based residential center. The theory underlying the Silverlake experiment was that delinquent behavior is not a private and secret deviation, but one in which others participate, share extensive knowledge, provide techniques, or give sanctions. To wit, it is behavior in a particular social context that attracts peers and gives status to its perpetrators.[37] As an intervention strategy, a mediatory community program was set up to avoid some of the negative aspects of institutional life. Staff members and residents attempted to create a nondelinquent culture in which those who reformed themselves were recognized and rewarded by their peers. Boys in the experimental program were allowed community contacts freely. They attended the local high school and returned to their own homes each weekend.[38] An experimental group and a control group were chosen from the inmate population of Boys Republic, situated in Los Angeles County. The experimental boys, aged 15 to 17, were lodged in a large house on the outskirts of downtown Los Angeles. The total number of boys at any one time never exceeded twenty; the size of the staff was also small. An experienced person, a bachelor, was hired as the director of the Silverlake experiment; he resided at the house. The program included a daily group meeting, attendance at school, some house-keeping chores, and tutorial activities. The daily meetings of boys were aimed at problem solving, using guided group interaction. The boys played ball in the evening and were allowed weekend visits home. The program remained in operation for a period of 32 months.

The experiment proved the following points in favor of community-based corrections: Treatment of delinquents in an open center presented little danger to the community. The rate of recidivism in the experimental group was about the same as in the institutional group. The operating costs of the open center were far less than those of the larger institution.[39]

The above two experiments at deinstitutionalization involved community-based *residential* centers. The next experiment involved the use of a nonresidential program.

Provo Experiment

A classic example of a nonresidential program is the Provo experiment.[40] The program was begun at Pinehills, Utah; it was designed to help habitual and persistent delinquents between the ages of 14 and 18 years. The experiment was based on the sociological premise that these habitual offenders were active members of a delinquent social system, and as such they would experience personal change if their group (the gang) changed its shared values and points of view. The group, accordingly, was to be the active change agent. The group was to play a major role in helping its members solve their problems and make basic decisions affecting participating members. It was also recognized that the project needed the community's active support for reintegration of the delinquent boys.

The experiment included only repeat offenders. After adjudication of each boy's case, the judge decided either to place the boy on probation or incarcerate him in a training school. Boys for the experimental group were chosen randomly from these two groups. Subjects in the experimental group were thus compared with two other groups—the probation group and the training school group.

The boys were exposed to the program for periods ranging from six to nine months. The subjects in the experimental group lived in their own homes. Some went to school, while others were employed in a paid city work program. On Saturdays, all the boys worked. Late in the afternoon of each day, the boys left school or work, went to Pinehills and attended a group meeting. These sessions were patterned on the technique of guided group interaction, emphasizing the idea that only through a group and its processes can a boy work out his problems. The group was powerful in the sense that it decided when each boy was ready to be released. These boys knew each other well, and it was difficult for them to hide their past activities or to fake improvement. Each boy had to confess all his delinquent acts and then analyze his feelings and attitudes in so doing. The group also had the authority to recommend to the court the transfer of a member to the state training school.

From a peer point of view, this procedure had three main goals:[41]

1. To question the utility of a life devoted to delinquency.
2. To suggest alternative behavior.
3. To provide recognition for a youngster's personal reformation and willingness to reform others.

The experimental group showed a more favorable evaluation, for both the short-term and the long-term. The experimental group had a mean arrest rate of 0.60 against 1.82 for the controls.[42] Six months after release, the experimental group showed a success rate of 84%, the probation group 77%, and the incarcerated group 42%. Furthermore, the most serious offenses were committed by escapees from incarceration, and not by the experimental subjects who never left the community.

The Provo experiment demonstrated that serious offenders can be treated in the community without posing unnecessary danger. However, a similar experiment, known as the Los Angeles Community Delinquency Control Project, did not show very encouraging results for the community-based group. Boys who succeed in one program may not succeed in another, and vice versa. Just as individuals differ, programs differ in their organization, setting, and content. The Los Angeles city boys may have had more difficulty in adjusting to their urban milieu than the Provo rural boys had.

Empey advises the proper matching of personal and organizational factors.[43] Comparing the residential (Silverlake experiment) and nonresidential (Provo experiment) programs, he found that the nonresidential program yields more desirable results. Moreover, "the experimental community program seemed to have a more lasting impact on those assigned to it than did the incarceration control program." According to Empey, just as local communities, families, and schools are likely to vary, correctional programs will have to vary in the way they operate.

A Radical Strategy: Closing of Training Schools

During the period 1971–72, the Division of Youth Services (DYS) of Massachusetts closed its juvenile correctional institutions.[44] Some of the events leading to this unprecedented and bold step will now be discussed.

Before 1969, the Massachusetts Division of Youth Services, like state correctional agencies in most states, relied on the use of youth training schools to handle a substantial number of their problem youths. The DYS training schools had the usual educational and vocational programs; however, these schools were basically custodial and authoritarian in nature with emphasis on conformity and obedience to rules. There were some reports of brutal and punitive treatment of youths which led to a series of investigations, studies, and recommendations. In the wake of all these inquiries, the director of DYS resigned and the board began a national search for a new director. The choice was Dr. Jerome Miller, who had the experience of organizing a new institution for disturbed or delinquent children of American Air Force personnel in England.

Commissioner Miller was an advocate of therapeutic communities designed by Maxwell Jones in England and Scotland. A therapeutic community is supposed to train residents of an institution for adjustment to social life and work conditions outside the institution. Participants of this community play an active role in changing themselves and also in helping their coparticipants in the growth process.[45] This treatment model requires a democratic atmosphere and staff and youths interact in small units. Youths are allowed to wear their own street clothes rather than institutional garments. They can also choose their hair style, a sensitive issue in the late 1960s. In fact, the youths are given every opportunity for self-expression, personal initiative, achievement, shared responsibility, a sense of belonging, and other socializing experiences.

Some staff members agreed with the philosophy of Commissioner Miller, others resisted his policies and sought to sabotage these new practices. The resulting discord was counterproductive to a healthy therapeutic community. Miller concluded that therapeutic communities could be run more successfully in small group homes located in the community—not in the institutions. He also felt that professional services for the youths could be provided more effectively in the community and that community-based group homes would attract more volunteers. Eventually, training schools were closed and youth were temporarily transferred to the University of Massachusetts for a month. Ironically, Massachusetts, which was one of the first states to start a training school in 1846, became the first to abolish such institutions.

Assisted by college students, who served as advocates for DYS youths, arrangements were made to place these deinstitutionalized youths in either group homes or in suitable foster homes. Many youths were placed in nonresidential programs close to their home communities. The community correctional programs emphasized establishing links between youths and public and private agencies which helped youths to find legitimate roles in the community. Neighborhood youth corps and the State Employment Agency were persuaded to supply jobs, YMCAs or YWCAs were requested to provide a place of residence, and public welfare agencies were asked to provide financial assistance. These community programs were dealing with real issues in the real world, which was different from the world of traditional training schools. This advocacy approach sought to assist communities to identify and develop services most needed by problem youths.

With respect to youth advocacy, Ohlin makes the following comments:[46]

> If resources are not available, appropriate agencies, service groups, or informal groups must be encouraged to develop them. If re-

sources exist, but are unavailable to the client, then actions must be taken to make them available. Examples of such advocacy include generating public concern for a class of clients such as drug users, intervening on behalf of a youngster with a vice-principal in a school, and mobilizing appropriate pressures and inducements for employers to permit the hiring of ex-offenders.

Unfortunately, reintegration and advocacy strategies have not been adequately implemented and studied.

RECIDIVISM.   After two years of deinstitutionalization in Massachusetts, preliminary recidivism data are available. Deinstitutionalization in Massachusetts did not result in a substantial increase in recidivism, but neither did it result in a substantial decrease. Region-by-region analysis shows rather dramatic shifts in both directions. These shifts cannot be explained at this stage. One fact which is clear from the Massachusetts experience is that it is possible to have a large number of youths in open settings without any increased danger to the community from recidivating youths.[47]

Interestingly, recidivism rates were more a function of region rather than that of offender characteristics. Regions which appeared to have aggressively implemented new programs needed by deinstitutionalized youths reduced their recidivism rates by about 50%. Regions which made little progress developing programs needed by these youths tended to detain more of these youths. Unfortunately, the decision by the juvenile court to detain youth proved to have an adverse influence on those detained.

> Whether or not a youth is detained prior to his court hearing even influences his likelihood of recidivating after release from a program, months later, holding constant his personal characteristics and the program intervention itself.[48]

The decision to detain seemed to be largely influenced by both where the youth lived and the policies of the court before which the youth appeared. These findings suggest that circumstances leading to a youth's detention, recidivism, and subsequent career in crime were the result of the community's reaction to the youth rather than just the behavior exhibited by these youth.

Recently, the Center for Criminal Justice, Harvard Law School, published a Series on Massachusetts Youth Correction Reforms. A study on *Designing Correctional Organizations for Youths: Dilemmas of Subcultural Development* points out that increased equality between inmates and staff and also between staff members is one of the first steps in efforts to achieve humanization and administrative control in juvenile centers. Increases in equality coincide with increases in mutual respect between staff members and youths. According to McEwen, the author of this study, the greater the community contacts in a program, the higher the level of equality. In addition, with the widening of community contacts, the center's residents transfer their interests to the community, thus losing interest in individual and group counseling administered at the center. This reduces the institutional staff's ability to alter the values of youths.[49] One of the major advantages of moving youths from large institutions to community-based programs is the wide diversity of alternative programs which become available to the staff and clients.

Community Treatment Project (CTP)

From 1961 to the middle of the 1970s, the California Youth Authority (CYA) has conducted a large scale, two-part experiment known as the Community Treatment Project.[50] Its basic goal was to determine if certain kinds of juvenile offenders could be allowed to remain in their home communities, if given intensive supervision and treatment within a small-sized parole caseload.

In the first part of the project (1961–1969), 852 boys and 212 girls between 13 and 19 years of age participated. All economic levels and racial backgrounds were represented. Some youths involved in violent crimes were excluded. The participants had been in trouble with the law on an average of five to eight occasions.

In order to compare the performance of youths placed directly into the intensive CTP program, without prior institutionalization, a "control" group of youths was sent to an institution for several months prior to being returned to their home communities, and prior to being given routine supervision within standard-sized parole caseloads operated by a different (non-CTP) group of parole agents. All eligible youths were randomly assigned to the two groups. Youths in the experimental group were supervised in small caseloads not exceeding 12 members. Based upon detailed initial interviews, a careful review of written background material and a joint conference by responsible CTP staff, a "treatment plan" was developed for each experimental youth. Another important measure on each youth was his "level of maturity." Youths of particular "levels of maturity" were paired with certain parole agents who possessed skills to deal with these types of youths. Seven out of every eight youths were included in three personality classifications: *(1)* passive conformist (14%), *(2)* power oriented (21%), and, *(3)* neurotic (53%).

RESULTS (1961–1969).   Those youths classified as neurotics performed much better within the intensive CTP program than within the traditional program. Controls were arrested 2.7 times more often than experimentals. Power-oriented youths who participated in the intensive CTP program performed substantially worse than those in the traditional program. Passive conformists in the CTP did better in terms of arrests, but worse in terms of convictions. A 24-month parole follow-up showed that experimental boys performed significantly better than control boys in terms of recidivism rate: 44% vs. 63%. Girls performed equally well in the traditional program and in the CTP. During the early years of the CTP, the traditional program was less expensive than the CTP, but in later years (in the 1970s), the cost-balance tipped in favor of the CTP program.

SECOND PHASE OF EXPERIMENT (1969–1974).   By 1967–1968, the CTP had found that at least one-third of youths were again involved in delinquency within a few weeks or months after having entered the program. This was true of both the experimentals and controls. Included within this broad "difficult-to-reach" category were some individuals from nearly all personality groupings. However, it was the difficult-to-reach neurotic who accounted for the largest total number. It was determined that those youths who did not do well in either the traditional or experimental program should be placed in a residential center known as Dorm 3. These residential centers housed about 20 to 25 youths who were supervised by youth counselors.

For empirical testing, youths who were seen as needing residential treatment were split in two groups. One group was given residential treatment, followed by parole supervision in the community. The other group was not given residential treatment. The group given residential treatment showed better results than the other group which indicated the need for residential treatment for youths denied this form of treatment. Fifty-eight percent of the youths provided residential treatment committed one or more offenses during 18 months of parole as compared to 94% of the control groups. These findings suggest that delinquent behavior of "hard-to-reach" youths may be substantially reduced if they are first exposed to a program such as provided by Dorm 3.

Palmer concluded[51] that delinquents need "differential treatment" and that "differential settings" are required for different groups of delinquents.

> . . . the CTP program does not contain a "special potion" which, after having been taken, is capable of eliminating all traces of delinquency. . . . Nevertheless, the "differential treatments" and "differential settings" which have been utilized in this program do seem capable of *reducing* the total volume of delinquent behavior on the part of many, but by no means all, eligible males. . . . In order to bring about this "reduction," it has very often seemed unnecessary to initially place these individuals within a residential setting (traditional or otherwise); in many other cases, it has seemed quite necessary. . . . It is what goes on *within* the given setting that seems to count, and not just the setting itself.

YOUTH SERVICE BUREAUS (YSB)

The President's Commission on Law Enforcement and Administration of Justice (1967) recommended establishment of youth service bureaus:[52]

> Communities should establish neighborhood youth-serving agencies—Youth Service Bureaus—located if possible in comprehensive neighborhood community centers and receiving juveniles (delinquent and nondelinquent) referred by the police, the juvenile court, parents, schools, and other sources.
>
> These agencies would act as central coordinators of all community services for young people and would also provide services lacking in the community or neighborhood, especially ones designed for less seriously delinquent juveniles.

In both theory and practice, the primary function of YSBs has been the diversion of problem youths from the juvenile justice system. However, these agencies also have the potential to play a major role in the deinstitutionalization of certain youths. Whether YSBs become a factor in the deinstitutionalization or diversion of youth will be contingent on their willingness to serve youth who are likely candidates for incarceration. Research studies indicate that YSBs have primarily served as supplements to the juvenile justice system rather than substitutes for it. This means many of the youth served by YSBs are youth who would probably never have entered this system.

The bulk of referrals to YSBs come from police, courts, schools, and parents. In order to encourage self-referrals, the bureaus have made their services accessible to young people through convenient locations and hours, by instituting hotlines and drop-in centers, and through the activities of outreach workers. Bureaus are being located near schools and business and commercial areas frequented by young people. Hotlines are being operated by sympathetic interns who are usually college students.

Many status offenders have been handled by YSBs. The bureau may render a particular service directly or refer youths to an appropriate agency. Some services may have to be purchased by the bureau for the youths. YSBs can arrange individual and family counseling with systematic follow-up and case conferences in complete confidentiality. Group programs developed by YSBs may include new approaches to youth–police relations, parent education, group activities, and group counseling. Youth shelters, street academies, group homes, and crisis centers may also be operated under the auspices of YSBs. These bureaus can function as youth advocates if their administrative structures allow them to do so. Services which may be arranged by YSBs are shown in Figure 5.1.

SUMMARY AND CONCLUSIONS

Despite some recent relaxation, the rate of incarceration for juveniles in the United States remains very high. In the early 1970s there were some indications that the populations of training schools were decreasing and that the numbers of youths served by community-based institutions were increasing. It is too early to determine if this is a trend or a temporary phenomenon. It is emphasized that the use of community-based institutions as supplements rather than substitutes for training schools has not resulted in deinstitutionalization. This practice results in many youth being committed to institutions at high costs to taxpayers. Although some large institutions (capacity of 500 or more) have been closed, the phasing out of training schools is not moving rapidly.

The National Advisory Commission on Criminal Justice Standards and Goals (1973) advised the nation to refrain from building more state institutions for juveniles and to phase out present institutions within a five-year period. It is realized that some dangerous delinquents will have to be kept in secure institutions for the protection of society, but most juveniles do not require secure institutions. Certainly status offenders do not deserve incarceration and should be deinstitutionalized. States vary greatly in

Youth Services Bureau

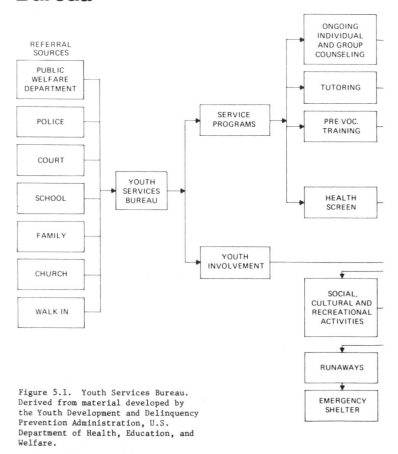

Figure 5.1. Youth Services Bureau.
Derived from material developed by
the Youth Development and Delinquency
Prevention Administration, U.S.
Department of Health, Education, and
Welfare.

rates of incarceration. Some states incarcerate 20 times more juveniles than other states, even though the juvenile crime rate is lower than in those states which refrain from placing a heavy reliance on institutions. Amazingly, more rural and less industrialized states rely more heavily on incarceration, although juven-

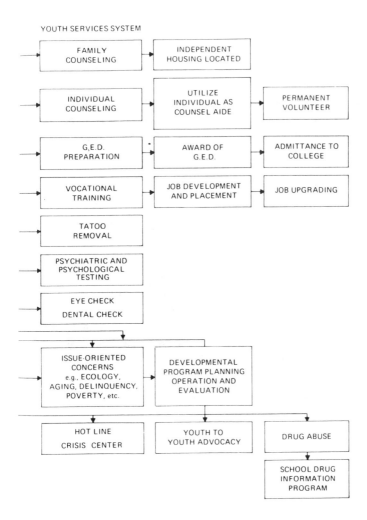

YOUTH SERVICES SYSTEM

ile delinquency is more a problem of urban areas. The dependence of some states on institutions to handle their problem youths has adverse consequences for both youths and taxpayers.

Security and custodial institutions can greatly harm their residents. Their negative effects have been investigated through observational and empirical studies. Street et al. found that institution characteristics override the inmates background traits. Thus, a security institution, with its custodial goals and the punitive attitude of its staff members, adversely affects inmates, regardless of their background.

Some states are moving toward community-based institutions, but to effect a saving in the total budget, a substantial portion of juvenile offenders must be placed in these community-based programs, accompanied by the closing of expensive, ineffective institutions.

Several experiments aimed at deinstitutionalization and measuring the effectiveness of alternative residential and nonresidential programs in the community have been analyzed. The Highfields experiment showed a lower rate of recidivism as compared to the reformatory. In the Silverlake experiment, the rate of recidivism in the experimental group was about the same as the institutional group, but the operating costs of the open center were far lower than those of the larger institution. Empey, who evaluated both the Silverlake (residential) and Provo (nonresidential) experiments, observed that the nonresidential program yielded more desirable results. Massachusetts took a radical step toward deinstitutionalization by closing down juvenile institutions and transferring youths to community-based residential and nonresidential programs. We have learned from the Massachusetts experience that it is possible to have a large number of youths in open settings without increasing danger to the community from recidivating youth. Circumstances leading to a youth's detention and recidivism in Massachusetts were posited in the community rather than in individual youth. Finally, the Community Treatment Project (CTP) of California tells us that intensive CTP programs (involving supervision in a small group) are good for neurotics, but not for power-oriented youths. Difficult youth initially need treatment in a special residential center followed by community supervision. The CTP Project indicates that no program is a panacea for all youths and that youths should be matched with programs appropriate to their needs.

OUTLINE FOR CHAPTER 6

Due Process Compliance: An Alternative to Denial of Due Process Protections

Due Process
    Definition
    Goals
Key U.S. Supreme Court Decisions Which Mandate Due Process for Juveniles
Juvenile Court Compliance with Due Process Requirements Mandated by the U.S. Supreme Court
Critical Elements Associated with the Implementation of Due Process for Juveniles
    Appeals
    Transcripts and Probation Reports
    Waiver and Transfer
    Detention Procedures
    Probation Review and Revocation
    Rules of Evidence
    Utilization of Defense Counsel
Rationales for the Failure of the Juvenile Court to Fully Comply with Due Process Requirements
Measurement of Due Process Compliance in the Juvenile Court
Actions Required to Augment Due Process Compliance in the Juvenile Court

Chapter 6

DUE PROCESS COMPLIANCE

An Alternative to Denial of Due Process Protections

DUE PROCESS

Definition

Due process may be defined as the presence in judicial proceedings of the traditional procedural safeguards guaranteed by the Bill of Rights in the U.S. Constitution, safeguards which protect individual liberties and restrict the action of the state.[1]

Goals

One goal of due process is to develop rules for conflict resolution which will ensure that a defendant has an opportunity, equal to the state, to present his case. The operation of the court may be viewed as a nonphysical conflict game between the state, which is represented by a prosecutor, and a defendant, who is represented by an attorney. Also present are a judge and jury who set rules of conduct and declare a winner. In theory, if both the prosecution and defense have an equal opportunity to present their client's case, the truth will emerge and the verdict and disposition will reflect this truth.

A second goal of due process is to ensure that the "unalienable rights" of U.S. citizens who come to trial are protected. To be free from illegal search and seizure and to remain silent are two such rights.

With respect to the juvenile court, procedural safeguards provided by the Bill of Rights are complex and are clouded by the ambiguity associated with the status of youths and their rights as people.[2]

KEY U.S. SUPREME COURT DECISIONS WHICH MANDATE DUE PROCESS FOR JUVENILES

Remarkably, constitutional issues surrounding the juvenile court, an agency of government, were not confronted by the U.S. Supreme Court until 66 years after the first juvenile court act. Since 1966, the Supreme Court has considered four significant cases which have had an important impact on the operation of the juvenile court. These cases include:

1. *Kent v. United States, 383 U.S. 541 (1966)*. This was the first juvenile court case decided in the Supreme Court of the United States. The Court affirmed that waiver hearings must "measure up to the essentials of due process and fair treatment." In Kent, the Supreme Court established that a standard of due process taken from the Fourteenth Amendment is applicable in the juvenile court. The Kent case may have established, in view of Gault's emphatic endorsement of Kent, a due process right that counsel have access to social and medical reports in the possession of the state, and furthermore, that a statement of reasons be given for court action.[3]

2. *In re Gault 387 U.S. 1 (1967)*. In this extremely important case, the Supreme Court held that fact-finding (adjudicatory) hearings were to be measured by due process standards. In all

cases, due process requires adequate, timely, written notice of the allegations against the respondent. Juveniles, in all cases in which they are in danger of loss of liberty because of commitment, are to be accorded, on due process grounds, the right to counsel, the privilege against self-incrimination, and the right to confront and cross examine witnesses under oath. The Gault case requires that a child and his/her parents be informed of his/her right to counsel and be told that, if they are unable to afford a lawyer, one will be appointed by the court. Gault states that juveniles need assistance of counsel to cope with problems of law, to make skilled inquiry into the facts, to insist upon the regularity of the proceedings, to ascertain whether he/she has a defense, and to prepare and submit a defense. 387 U.S. at 36.[4]

 3. *In re Winship, 397 U.S. 358 (1970).* This case held that, in some delinquency proceedings, juveniles, like adults, are entitled to a standard of proof beyond a reasonable doubt. As in Gault, the opinion in Winship is limited to the adjudicatory state of a delinquency proceeding in which the respondent may be committed to a state institution.[5]

 [Paulsen opines that Kent, Gault, and Winship, when read together, indicate that procedures essential to fairness ought not be discarded because of rehabilitative aims and beneficient purposes, and that the fundamentals of due process will not, in truth, stand in the way of any legitimate goal of the courts for children.[6]]

 4. *McKeiver v. Pennsylvania, 403 U.S. 528 (1971).* This case held that a juvenile is not constitutionally entitled to the right of trial by jury. The opinion of the Court is based, in part, on the concern that, if jury trials were required in adjudicatory proceedings, the proceedings would become indistinguishable from criminal trials. This opinion asserts that much good is still to be found in the traditional insistence upon an informal "non adversary" hearing.[7]

 In these four cases, the Supreme Court indicated that it wants to retain some of the informality of the juvenile justice system, with the alleged benefits thereof, while ensuring an atmosphere orderly enough to impress juveniles with the gravity of the situation and the impartiality of the tribunal. As should be expected, disappointment with the juvenile court system continues, and numerous state courts and lower federal courts are applying the broad principles of Gault to many issues not yet decided by the U.S. Supreme Court.[8]

JUVENILE COURT COMPLIANCE WITH DUE PROCESS REQUIREMENTS MANDATED BY THE U.S. SUPREME COURT

To have an effect, a legal mandate must first achieve compliance. Although many persons assume that mandating an action will result in compliant behavior, much evidence in social science literature reveals that this is not the case.[9] The National Assessment of Juvenile Corrections (NAJC) made the following findings with regard to the degree to which juvenile courts comply with due process requirements mandated by the U.S. Supreme Court:

Mandate: As required by Winship, the juvenile court shall use the criterion of proof beyond a reasonable doubt in making adjudication decisions.

Compliance: Although 95% of judges in the NAJC survey reported that they use "proof beyond a reasonable doubt," only 52% of said judges affirmed that they *never* have access to youths social files before adjudication. This means there is a strong probability that a high percentage of judges, at some hearings, violate the spirit of the law mandated in Winship in that they use potentially compromising material before making a decision about a youth rather than using a standard of proof based only on evidence.

Mandate: As required by Gault, the juvenile court shall provide written notice of charges to youths.

Compliance: The NAJC reports that 90% of responding judges declare that written notice of charges is always given to defendants. However, only 68% of these courts present the notice in both statutory language and factual allegations. This means that a large percentage of youths may receive a notice of charges against them which are deficient in that the youth or his parents may be unable to understand said charges (only statutory language), or may not include all the information required by the youth's counsel (only factual information).

Mandate: As required by Gault and Kent, the juvenile court shall, at both adjudication (Gault) and waiver (Kent) hearings, inform juveniles that they have a right to counsel and that counsel will be appointed by the court if the defendant cannot afford to pay for an attorney.

Compliance: Ninety-seven percent of reporting judges indicate that juveniles have a right to counsel at adjudication hearings, and 86% of these judges report that, when necessary, counsel is appointed at such hearings. In regard to waiver hearings, 86% of the judges report a right to counsel, and only 77% will appoint counsel if needed. Twelve percent of the judges indicate that they seldom appoint attorneys at any stage of juvenile court proceedings.

Mandate: As required by Gault, the juvenile court shall provide the defendant with the right to confront and cross examine witnesses.

Compliance: Eighty-seven percent of responding courts in the NAJC survey apparently follow state rules of evidence which implies the ability to confront evidence. Attorney access to a youth's social file was reported by 72% of judges, whereas 86% of courts allow lawyers to call witnesses named in the social report.[10]

CRITICAL ELEMENTS ASSOCIATED WITH THE IMPLEMENTATION OF DUE PROCESS FOR JUVENILES

Frequency of appeals in juvenile court proceedings, prevalence of formal transcripts and probation reports, the extent to which caes are waived to adult court, procedures which govern detention of youths, regularity with which probation cases are reviewed, application of rules of evidence in adjudication hearings, and the utilization of defense counsel are critical elements related to the implementation of due process. Following is a discussion of these elements.

Appeals

The right to appeal a juvenile court determination is not a constitutional right; it is created by statute. The issue of a federal constitutional appeal in juvenile cases, based on due process of law, was expressly left open in In re Gault, 387 U.S. 1 (1967). Furthermore, many state court opinions aver that the right to a review of juvenile court proceedings is not essential to due process of law, but is a matter of grace.[11] Finally, in spite of the technical nature of an appeal raising questions beyond a lay person's ability to resolve, few state statutes provide for counsel on appeal. Provision for payment for counsel appointed for an appeal is most unusual. Paulsen opines that a constitutional right to appeal may well be recognized in juvenile cases on equal protection grounds, as has occurred in adult criminal cases (Douglas v. California, 372 U.S. 353 (1963)), and because it would be a logical extension of Gault. Paulsen also asserts that states which provide for appellate review should do so only with the provision of fairness which a right to counsel gives. See, e.g., Chambers v. District Court, 261 Iowa 31, 152 N.W. 2d 818 (1967).[12]

In California, from the inception of its juvenile court in 1906 until 1960, an average of two cases were appealed annually.[13] The National Assessment of Juvenile Corrections further confirms that appeals are a rare occurrence in juvenile court. Fifty-eight percent of the judges in the national survey reported that they had no appeals the previous year. Of the 120 courts with appeals, the median number of appeals was three. Sixty-five percent of the judges which had cases appealed indicated that they had no information about the cases appealed. Only 1% of the judges reported an automatic right of appeal.[14] In only 30 states are appeals taken to an appellate court or directly to the state supreme court.[15]

Review by an appellate court indicates that the juvenile court has status equal to that of the highest trial court in the state.[16] Sarri states that the appeal process may be the only kind of enforcement to which juvenile court judges are susceptible, given this country's tradition of an independent judiciary. As long as cases are appealed, judges cannot indefinitely disregard the correct application of a law or legal procedure; their decisions will eventually be reversed.[17]

The President's Crime Commission on Law Enforcement and the Administration of Justice Task Force on Juvenile Delinquency expressed the opinion that the lack of appellate surveillance on the juvenile court has adversely affected the quality of juvenile justice in the following ways:[18]

1. There has been no appellate forum to rectify errors and injustices in particular cases.

2. The juvenile justice system has been deprived of the kind of sustained examination and formulation of law and policy that appellate review can provide.

3. It has not been possible to develop, through appellate review, uniform application of a law throughout a state.

Transcripts and Probation Reports

Paulsen states that sufficiently detailed records of trial court proceedings must be available if appellate review is to perform its function properly. Few juvenile court statutes require that a transcript be filed or that records be transferred to an appellate court.[19]

Transcripts and records are important to appeals of juvenile court decisions because such information is frequently the only basis upon which an appeal can be made. Moreover, the existence of transcripts and records of juvenile court proceedings determine the direction of an appeal. To illustrate, assuming a statute provides for an appeal to the state supreme court, the *lack* of a transcript may result in the appeal having to be made to a court of record (horizontal appeal) rather than to an appellate court (vertical appeal).[20]

The NAJC survey found that only 59% of responding judges had transcripts for adjudicatory hearings with nearly the same percentage for disposition hearings and hearings for dependency and neglect cases. Only 4% of the courts studied used tape recordings instead of transcripts. Sarri suggests that the 20% success rate of appeals of juvenile court cases may be attributed to the absence of adequate transcripts. These data document that the ability of appellate or supreme courts to assess performance of persons who serve as judges in the juvenile court is severely limited.[21]

With regard to the availability or use of probation reports, 75% of the judges in the NAJC survey responded that probation reports are always open to challenge, and that defense attorneys have access to a juvenile's social file. Although a relatively high percentage of judges indicated that they permit probation reports to be challenged, 14% of these judges said that either juveniles or their attorneys are *not* permitted to obtain the names of those supplying information so they can call them as witnesses at adjudication. This is unfortunate since the availability or use of probation reports facilitates the role of counsel in ensuring due process to juveniles.[22]

Waiver and Transfer

Nearly all states allow a juvenile court judge to waive jurisdiction and transfer a juvenile to the adult criminal justice system for adjudication or disposition. Only 36 states have set a minimum age below which juveniles may not be waived to an adult court.[23] Such states as Alaska, New Hampshire, and South Dakota allow the juvenile court to waive jurisdiction no matter what the child's age.[24]

The NAJC survey found that waiver of juveniles to adult court occurred in about 55% of the reporting courts. When waiver did occur, 50% of reporting judges responded that they lacked information about action subsequent to the waiver decision. This lack of information concerning outcomes of waiver decisions prevents judges from determining whether or not their waiver decisions serve the interests of youths or the community. In decisions involving the transfer of a youth from a probationary status to a state instution, NAJC survey respondents reported that hearings were held 88% of the time. Conversely, court hearings were seldom held for youths transferred from state juvenile facilities to adult correctional facilities since, in most states, authority for such transfers rests with a state administrative agency rather than the court.[25]

The transfer of a youth from the juvenile to the adult court is actually a kind of pretrial disposition, a disposition which can have grave consequences for a youth since the conditions of incarceration may be extremely harsh, the length of sentence excessive, and the exposure to adult felons increases the likelihood the youth will become a career criminal.[26]

Depending on one's viewpoint, the transfer of a youth from the juvenile court to the punitive criminal justice system may be a safety valve or cop-out. Proponents of the transfer system argue that some youth are so vicious, so hardened, or have performed acts of such shocking criminality as to evidence complete unamenability to treatment. They maintain that society is in just as great a need of protection from these youths as from their adult counterparts. On the other hand, others claim that the existence of such loopholes in the juvenile justice system indicates a half-hearted commitment to treatment and a continued allegiance to retribution on the part of society, an allegiance which is especially distasteful when applied to the very persons whom the separate juvenile court was designed to protect.[27]

Detention Procedures

More than one million youths are held in juvenile detention and adult jails each year.[28] A large number of states do not lay down legislative criteria which justify the detention of a youth after arrest. In some states, statutes provide that a juvenile must be accorded a prompt hearing to inquire into the reason for continued detention. In other states, youths may be detained upon a court order with no expressed provision for a hearing.[29] There is a body of opinion in lower courts which recognizes, on constitutional grounds, a right to a detention hearing and a decision based on adequate evidence. Some of these cases indicate that the detention of youths must be justified on a finding of probable cause that the youth committed an offense.[30]

The NAJC survey indicated that 49% of reporting juvenile judges believed that placing a youth in a detention center or adult jail is a good way to show him/her the court means business. Only 48% of judges "always or often" based probable cause related to an allegation as the criterion for the detention of youths. Protection of the juvenile (70%) and protection of the community (66%) were the criteria most used always or often by judges to detain a youth. The survey also indicated that judges (94%), probation officers, (51%), intake workers (39%), referees (28%), and police (20%) may admit youths to detention.

With regard to the conduct of hearings for detention, in 47% of the detention centers studied, the detention center directors reported that detention hearings were conducted within 48 hours in less than 10% of the cases. Just 42% of detention directors indicated that judges always reviewed detention decisions.[31]

The NAJC survey showed that alternatives to detention most frequently used by reporting judges were:

1. Release to parents (93%).
2. Release of youth on his/her own recognizance (42%).
3. Foster or shelter care (36%).
4. Bail (7%).[32]

A constitutional right to bail for juveniles has not been recognized.[33] Although 20 states permit posting of bail, the NAJC survey indicates that in some of these states judges do not allow juveniles to post it.[34]

Probation Review and Revocation

Only seven states now require a periodic review of probation cases, whereas seven other states place a time limit on the probation period. Interestingly, New York has established a shorter probation period for status offenders than for delinquents.[35]

Judges and probation officers in the NAJC survey concurred that a review of probation cases was infrequent. Ninety-four percent of judges responded that probation termination was based "very often" or "often" on the recommendation of the probation officer. Thirty-nine percent of judges and 46% of probation officers reported "very often" or "often" using the definite sentence set by the judge as a criterion for the length of probation.

With respect to probation revocation, 89% of judges in the NAJC survey indicated that they always have hearings.[36]

Rules of Evidence

In adult courts, it is expected that a state's rules of evidence will always be followed.[37] In juvenile courts, no state requires the juvenile court judge to follow rules of evidence in admitting information about the alleged offense.[38] The NAJC survey indicated that 93% of full-time and 64% of part-time judges always follow rules of evidence in juvenile court. Responses to other survey items about hearings and adjudication decision-making suggest that formal rules often are secondary to informality and perceptions of the needs and capability of the juvenile.[39]

Utilization of Defense Counsel

Prior to Kent and Gault, a number of states provided a right to counsel, including court appointed counsel.[40] The right to counsel, in one form or another, is now statutorily guaranteed in all but 11 states.[41] Some states furnish youth counsel, including court appointed counsel, at all stages of juvenile court proceedings. Other states simply provide that a juvenile is entitled to be represented by counsel, without specifying whether it applies to all forms of conduct for which a youth might be before the court. Still other states provide for a more limited right to counsel in that they require the court to appoint counsel only when the youth requests counsel and is financially unable to retain counsel of his own choice, whereas other states permit the judge to use his discretion regardihg the appointment of counsel. Some states indicate the right to counsel is applicable to both delinquency cases and cases in which status offenses are alleged. Finally, some states provide that a youth has a right to be represented by counsel in neglect or dependency proceedings. Some states also provide that, in neglect or dependency proceedings, the parent is entitled to counsel, which includes court appointed counsel if the parent cannot afford retained counsel. In any event, in whatever form counsel might be provided, or whether provision is made by statute for representation by counsel at all, a juvenile is entitled to the assistance of counsel as a matter of constitutional due process. Notice to that effect and notice that counsel will be appointed to represent him if he cannot afford counsel are also required by due process.[42]

Judges in the NAJC survey indicate that juveniles should have a right to counsel at adjudication (97%), disposition (96%), and probation review or revocation (93%). These judges were far less likely to acknowledge a youth's right to counsel at detention (86%) and intake (69%) hearings. In all cases, the NAJC observed that at all stages of case processing, a lower proportion of judges arranged for the appointment of counsel when needed than acknowledged a youth's right to counsel.[43]

The NAJC determined that when lawyers were appointed in juvenile court, the activity of most of them appeared to be minimal. Only about 50% of judges report that lawyers "always" confront witnesses. Furthermore, only 20% of judges indicate that lawyers "often" call witnesses named in reports concerning their respective cases. Judges also report that very few motions are made by lawyers in juvenile court.[44] Nearly 50% of the responding courts indicate that no appeals of cases were made by lawyers in 1973. Field observations of juvenile courts by the NAJC indicate that attorneys tend to prefer to plea bargain with the judge on small points rather than on the adjudication itself. For example, some lawyers requested judges to drop three counts on a petition contingent on the youth admitting guilt on three counts. Since once a youth is adjudicated delinquent, the number of counts alleged in a petition makes no legal difference with regard to the disposition made, judges would often agree with such an arrangement.[45]

The foregoing data clearly indicate that, although there is almost a complete theoretical existence of counsel in the juvenile court, defense lawyers generally do not assume an active role in juvenile court hearings.[46] This is especially unfortunate in light of NAJC survey findings which show that in courts where judges perceived attorneys to have high influence, the following occurred:

1. Cases were appealed twice as often.
2. Motions were made more frequently.
3. Social reports were more accessible to defense attorneys and to parents, and were ultimately less accessible to judges before disposition decisions.
4. Judges showed greater concern with the protection of youths' rights and toward the rights of parents.
5. Criteria at adjudication related more to allegations against the youth than to the needs and capabilities of the youth.
6. The right to counsel was exercised throughout all stages of juvenile court proceedings.

Finally, although the NAJC survey did not indicate that a high level of activity by defense counsel would guarantee a greater attention to due process, the survey did show that the greater the influence of defense counsel in juvenile court, the more conditions associated with due process were likely to exist.[47]

RATIONALES FOR THE FAILURE OF THE JUVENILE COURT TO FULLY COMPLY WITH DUE PROCESS REQUIREMENTS

Rosemary Sarri, Co-director, National Assessment of Juvenile Corrections, describes the complex and varied responses of the juvenile court to due process demands as ambivalent. Although judges in the NAJC survey agree with the general idea of providing legal safeguards in juvenile court and often attempt to bring courtroom procedure in line with Supreme Court mandates in both ideology and practice, said judges often ensure that such protections do not go "too far" in altering the operation of the court. Among reporting judges, there were significant differences of opinions about what due process should involve. To illustrate, there is near unanimity among judges that some type of due process is important in the juvenile court; however, nearly one-third of responding judges did not "agree" or "strongly agree" with the statement that juvenile cases should be dismissed if there is insufficient evidence to substantiate an allegation, a basic premise of Supreme Court decisions.[48]

Duffee and Siegel suggest that the ambivalent responses of the juvenile court to U.S. Supreme Court mandates have resulted because the Supreme Court's message has been distorted to fit organizational needs. In other words, values and issues relevant to the Supreme Court are not sufficient to offset the rewards that govern the behavior of organizational officials. Furthermore, values important to the Supreme Court are not the primary criteria used to evaluate the performance of juvenile courts.[49]

According to Siegel, changing organizational behavior within the juvenile justice system is a complex process because techniques utilized in redrafting a law or reinterpreting a constitutional issue are not, by themselves, successful techniques for changing human behavior. By issuing an opinion that a juvenile has a right to counsel in waiver and adjudication hearings, the Supreme Court can establish the minimally acceptable standards that govern certain behavior in an organization. However, it is a common fact of organizational behavior that the rules prescribing the *minimal* effort required become the norm. The people who do the actual work of the system punish their peers for deviating from the norm in either direction. Consequently, if agency officials are motivated only by Supreme Court mandates or administrative policy, they are likely to obey the letter, not the spirit of the law.[50]

A study conducted by Lefstein, Stapleton, and Teitelbaum supports Siegel's commentary. This study involved researchers observing numerous court hearings in three urban courts for the purpose of determining compliance of the juvenile court with due process requirements mandated by Gault. Results of this study indicated that in over half of the cases observed, juveniles were not fully advised of their right to counsel, and were almost always advised of the right to counsel in a manner which discouraged their exercising this right. This was usually accomplished by framing or uttering a question with such emphasis, or accompanied by such nonverbal conduct of the questioner, as to suggest the desired answer. Furthermore, youths observed in court were usually not advised of their privilege against self-incrimination and the advice of the court regarding this privilege was invariably communicated in a prejudicial manner.[51]

MEASUREMENT OF DUE PROCESS COMPLIANCE IN THE JUVENILE COURT

The NAJC survey found that the average juvenile court only complies with about 70% of the due process requirements of U.S. Supreme Court decisions.[52] Reasons for this lack of compliance have already been promulgated.

The NAJC and others have demonstrated that due process compliance of a juvenile court can be measured. Indicators which might be utilized to measure due process compliance may include, but are not necessarily limited to, the following:

1.   Written notice of charges is always provided to youths and is always stated in both factual and statutory language.

2.   The court always uses the criterion of proof beyond a reasonable doubt in adjudication hearings.

3.   Hearings are always held before a youth is waived to an adult court.

4.   The court always uses a state's rules of evidence at adjudication hearings.

5.   The juvenile court judge never has access to social files at the adjudication hearing.

6. Juveniles always have a right to counsel at intake, detention, waiver, adjudication, disposition, and probation violation hearings.

7. Counsel is always appointed for juveniles at intake, detention, waiver, adjudication, disposition, and probation revocation hearings.

8. Only counsel can waive a youth's right to self-incrimination.

9. Counsel may always have access to a youth's social file, and always may call witnesses from the social report.

10. Counsel frequently calls witnesses from the youth's social report and usually cross examines witnesses.

11. Parents always have access to their child's social file.

12. The juvenile court judge reviews probation cases routinely and probation reports are always open to challenge.

13. Police, intake workers, detention staff, probation officers, and service agencies are prohibited from admitting youth to detention.

14. The juvenile court judge always uses probable cause as primary criterion in regard to his/her decision to detain a youth.

15. Probation revocation hearings are always held, and hearings are always held when juveniles are transferred from a juvenile to an adult correctional institution.

16. Hearings are always held with regard to changing the disposition of a case.

17. Court orders are never modified without a hearing.

18. The juvenile court always makes taped transcripts of intake, detention, waiver, adjudication, disposition, probation violation, dependency, and neglect hearings and, upon the request of defense counsel, always makes these transcripts available to counsel.

19. The juvenile court provides bail for youths or utilizes adequate substitutes for bail which include making every possible effort to place youths in situations where their freedom will not be curtailed.[53]

ACTIONS REQUIRED TO AUGMENT DUE PROCESS COMPLIANCE IN THE JUVENILE COURT

The failure of juvenile courts to fully comply with due process requirements mandated by the U.S. Supreme Court and to afford children and youth due process protections which are logical extensions of Supreme Court decisions has been documented. This unfortunate and inequitable situation can be improved if local advocacy groups (see Chapter 7) will influence state legislatures to enact laws which increase the likelihood that due process rights of children and youth will be protected, support the election and appointment of persons highly qualified by training and experience to serve as judges, prosecutors, and defense counsel in the juvenile court, and monitor due process compliance in the court.

To increase due process compliance in the juvenile court, state laws must be ratified which require the following:

1.   Written notice of charges against juveniles.

2.   Provision of counsel to juveniles at *all* stages of court proceedings.

3.   Adherence to state rules of evidence in the juvenile court which is required in adult criminal proceedings.

4.   Taped transcripts of all adjudication and dispositional hearings in juvenile court and the availability of these transcripts to defense counsel.

5.   Automatic right of appeal for juveniles and the provision of counsel at appellate hearings.

To enhance the chances that laws which require the aforesaid due process protections will be fully complied with, it will be necessary for persons who serve as judges, prosecutors, and defense attorneys in the juvenile court to have a due process orientation and to be highly qualified by training and experience. Therefore, local advocacy groups should support the election and appointment of persons to serve in these positions who state their intent to ensure that juveniles are provided all due process rights mandated by the Supreme Court, as well as those due process protections which are logical extensions of Supreme Court decisions. Furthermore, juvenile court judges, prosecutors and defense counsel, prior to their appointment or election, should have experience working with youths and possess, in addition to a law degree, a graduate degree in a human services area. If it is necessary for local communities to supplement emoluments for these positions to recruit persons with the foregoing qualifications, this should be done.

Finally, local advocacy groups can monitor due process compliance by observing juvenile court hearings and using due process indicators previously specified to measure the degree to which children and youth receive due process protections in the juvenile court.

If the aforesaid actions are implemented, organizational structures and interaction patterns should be developed in which juvenile justice officials will be positively rather than negatively reinforced for providing children and youths due process protections. Furthermore, it is hoped that in juvenile court jurisdictions where these actions are taken, juvenile justice officials will begin to fully embrace the due process model of a juvenile court and assume a philosophical position so eloquently stated by Rubin:[54]

> The juvenile court is a legal forum upon which social services have been grafted; it is not a social agency empowered with authority. The standards embodied in the law and the Constitution will serve us better than good intentions or rehabilitative enthusiasm. Due process-fairness is the best teacher and the best approach to securing client acceptance of our norms. Due process and rehabilitation are mutually reinforcing. Social judgments should not replace legal judgements in a court of law. We need to reeducate ourselves to the presumption of innocence which cloaks our child clients. We need to avoid the civil–criminal debate on the nature of our court. The issue is freedom. Freedom can be constrained or removed only through due process of law.

Without an acceptance of the due process model of a juvenile court, juvenile justice officials, particularly judges, will continue to be vested with unquestioned power over the lives of children and youths. How long will citizens allow such power to go unchecked? Is any man or woman wise enough or good enough to be trusted with such unbridled and arbitrary power?

OUTLINE FOR CHAPTER 7

Power Advocacy: A Vehicle for Making Juvenile Justice More Effective and Accountable

Power Advocacy in Juvenile Justice
  Definition
  Organization
  Implementation
  Operating Assumptions
The Need for Power Advocacy in Juvenile Justice
  The Failure of Traditional Advocacy in Juvenile Justice
  Isolation of the Juvenile Court
  Pressing Needs of Youth and the Juvenile Justice System which Require Power Advocacy
Four Reasons for the Efficacy of Power Advocacy in Juvenile Justice
  The Environments of the Juvenile Court and the Network of Agencies with which it Interacts are Vulnerable to Power Advocacy
  A Locality will Perceive the Need for Power Advocacy in Juvenile Justice
  Influential Local Groups and Organizations will Determine that They will Derive Benefits from the Implementation of Power Advocacy in Juvenile Justice
  The Impact of Power Advocacy in Juvenile Justice can be Measured
Implications of Power Advocacy in Juvenile Justice for State Youth Service Bureaucracies
A Final Comment

Chapter 7

POWER ADVOCACY

A Vehicle for Making Juvenile Justice More Effective and Accountable

POWER ADVOCACY IN JUVENILE JUSTICE

Definition

Power advocacy in juvenile justice would exist where the residents of a locality served by a juvenile court have the capability to expeditiously eliminate, modify, merge, expand, create, monitor, evaluate, and investigate delinquency prevention and control policies, programs, and practices because said residents are organized so as to possess the influence, authority, and expertise necessary to exercise the amount of control required over the environments of the juvenile court and the agencies with which the court interacts to perform the aforesaid tasks.

Organization

In order for citizens in a locality to successfully implement power advocacy in juvenile justice, it is essential that those local forces which influence the inputs, technology, outputs, and goal setting of that locality's juvenile court, and the youth service agencies with which the court interacts, create an organizational structure which is capable of exerting substantial control over the environments of the aforesaid youth service organizations. Those forces which have the most potential for influencing the activities of the juvenile court and agencies with which the court has transactions are major local public and private sources of funding for these agencies, (i.e., city and county government units, United Way, etc.) consumers of youth services, youth service agencies, and members of civic, service and religious organizations interested in delinquency prevention and control activities.

An organizational structure which can be used to implement power advocacy in juvenile justice in a locality is shown in Figure 7.1. The components of this structure and the respective properties of these components are as follows:

1. *City Government, County Government, and Major Sources of Funding for Private Youth Service Agencies.*

a. Appoint persons to serve on the Advocacy Commission for Children and Youth (ACCY).

b. Provide funding for the operation of the ACCY.

c. Direct all youth service agencies which seek to prevent and control juvenile delinquency, and which receive funding from appointing bodies, to fully cooperate with the ACCY.

d. Fund only those delinquency prevention and control programs approved by the ACCY, in consultation with its advisory committees, and eliminate, modify, merge, expand, and/or create delinquency prevention and control policies, programs, and procedures as recommended by the ACCY.

e. When recommended by the ACCY, appointing bodies request state and federal officials to eliminate, modify, merge, expand, and/or create delinquency prevention and control policies, programs, and practices.

2. *Advocacy Commission for Children and Youth.*

a. Speaks with one voice with regard to delinquency prev-

Figure 7.1

An Organizational Structure Designed to Implement

Power Advocacy in Juvenile Justice in a

Locality Served by a Juvenile Court

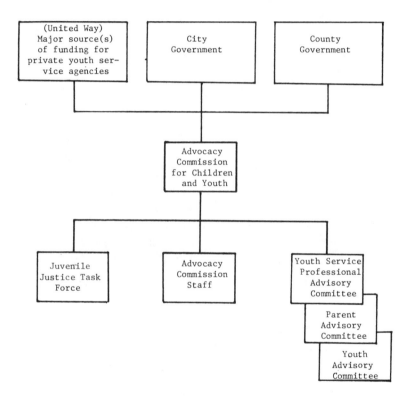

ention and control policies, programs, and practices which will be utilized in a locality served by a juvenile court.

b.   Functions as a private nonprofit corporation which receives funding from public and private sources, and has legitimacy because it is appointed by both elected local officials, who represent major sources of funding for public youth service agencies, and officials which represent organizations on which private youth service agencies are most dependent for financial resources.

c. Has a membership which is limited to adults who have demonstrated an interest in youth, and who have some political influence, but who are not affiliated with any public or private youth service organization.

d. Appoints professional youth service, youth and parent advisory committees, and consults these committees regarding all proposals related to the prevention and control of delinquency which are considered by the ACCY.

e. Receives authorization from its appointing bodies to: *(1)* make recommendations regarding the elimination, modification, merger, expansion, or creation of those service programs which have as a major objective the prevention and/or control of juvenile delinquency, and which are funded by the bodies which appoint the ACCY; *(2)* obtain and disseminate information to the community and government about specific services provided by all public and private youth service agencies in a locality served by a juvenile court and to disclose the annual cost of operating these service programs; *(3)* monitor and evaluate all delinquency prevention and control services on an ongoing basis; *(4)* investigate *all* youth service delivery problems reported to the ACCY, and to recommend actions to remediate those problems identified; *(5)* engage in litigation to rectify abuses in systems serving youth; and *(6)* employ a technical staff which has a high degree of competence in administration, program planning and implementation, evaluation research, negotiation, and litigation.

f. Recruits persons who are members of religious, service, and civic organizations to serve on a juvenile justice task force for the purpose of furnishing broad-based political and financial support for actions recommended by the ACCY.

3. *Youth Service Professional Advisory Committee.*

a. Has a membership which includes a minimum of one representative from all public and private agencies in a locality which seeks to prevent and control juvenile delinquency.

b. Informs the ACCY about problems related to the delivery of delinquency prevention and control services.

c. Evaluates proposals submitted to the ACCY regarding the elimination, modification, merger, expansion, or creation of delinquency prevention and control policies, programs, and practices.

4. *Parent Advisory Committee.*

a. Has a membership which includes parents who have a minimum of one child between 10 and 17 years of age, and who have not been employed by a youth service agency during a 12-month period preceding their appointment to this committee.

b. Informs the ACCY about problems related to the delivery of delinquency prevention and control services.

c. Evaluates proposals submitted to the ACCY regarding the elimination, modification, merger, expansion, or creation of delinquency prevention and control policies, programs, and practices.

5. *Youth Advisory Committee.*

a. Has a membership which is restricted to youths who are between 12 and 17 years of age, and which includes some youths who have been consumers of delinquency prevention and control services.

b. Informs the ACCY about problems related to the delivery of delinquency prevention and control services.

c. Evaluates proposals submitted to the ACCY regarding the elimination, modification, merger, expansion, or creation of delinquency prevention and control policies, programs, and practices.

6. *Juvenile Justice Task Force.*

a. Has a membership which includes members of those service, civic, and religious organizations which have demonstrated an interest in youth.

b. Has a membership which is highly informed about the operation of those agencies which seek to deliver delinquency prevention and control services and the consumers of these services.

c. Has a membership which includes persons who are interested in serving as members of the ACCY and who are willing to prepare themselves to serve in this capacity.

d. Constitutes a broad base of political and economic support for the ACCY.

Implementation

Following is a description of procedures which citizens can employ to implement power advocacy in juvenile justice in a locality served by a juvenile court.

FORM AN AD HOC COMMITTEE. One or more persons familiar with the operation of the juvenile justice system in their locality, and who are cognizant of some of the problems associated with the delivery of delinquency prevention and control services in that locality, should identify approximately 15 local persons who are interested in their community making more progress toward preventing and controlling delinquency. Those persons identified should have previously demonstrated an interest in youths and have some influence with members of local public and private groups which are major sources of funding for youth service organizations. To preclude a possible conflict of interest, none of those persons identified should be affiliated with a youth service organization.

When a sufficient number of persons with the afore described qualifications have been identified, they should be requested to serve on an ad hoc committee for the purpose of studying the feasibility of implementing power advocacy in juvenile justice in their locality.

MOTIVATE THE AD HOC COMMITTEE. Since persons requested to serve on the ad hoc committee probably will not have a comprehensive understanding of the operation of juvenile justice in their locality, they will need to participate in an orientation program. The orientation program should include such activities as:

1. Reviewing studies of efforts to prevent and control ju-

venile delinquency and viewing films concerning problems in juvenile justice. These materials can be obtained from both the National Criminal Justice Reference Service, an agency of the U.S. Law Enforcement Assistance Administration, and university libraries.

2. Observing juvenile court hearings and the operation of *all* those agencies which claim to provide delinquency prevention and control services. Personnel and clients at these agencies should be questioned about these service programs.

3. Determining whether power advocacy in juvenile justice as promulgated herein can be adapted to their community.

This orientation experience should prepare ad hoc committee members to pinpoint problems in juvenile justice and to come to an understanding of how power advocacy can remediate these problems. Furthermore, committee members should be able to effectively communicate this information to officials of public and private organizations which are major sources of funding for youth service organizations.

SECURE THE APPOINTMENT OF AN ADVOCACY COMMISSION FOR CHILDREN AND YOUTH. Once all members of the ad hoc committee have completed their orientation program, appropriate committee members should be assigned the task of meeting with each official of those local public and private organizations that serve as major sources of funding for agencies in the locality which seek to prevent and control juvenile delinquency. These meetings should be held for the purpose of persuading these officials to use their influence to implement power advocacy in juvenile justice in their locality. Once a majority of the representatives of major public and private funding sources of youth service agencies have agreed to support the use of power advocacy in juvenile justice, the ad hoc committee should draft a resolution for approval by these funding organizations. This resolution should include, as a minimum, the following:

1. Rationales for the creation of the ACCY.
2. Needs the ACCY will address and authorities which

public and private funding organizations appointing ACCY members will delegate to the ACCY to meet these needs.

3.   Amount of public and private funds which organizations appointing ACCY members will expend to finance the operation of the ACCY.

4.   Qualifications which persons must possess in order to be eligible for appointment to the ACCY.

In order to enhance the chances that the ACCY will perform in an auspicious fashion from its inception, the ad hoc committee should make a concerted effort to have ad hoc committee members appointed to the ACCY. Members of the juvenile justice task force established by the initial ACCY should be strongly considered as future appointees to the ACCY.

ORGANIZE THE ADVOCACY COMMISSION FOR CHILDREN AND YOUTH.   After the ACCY has been appointed, it should:

1.   Have appointees to the ACCY who were not members of the ad hoc committee successfully complete the same type orientation program as was completed by ad hoc committee members.

2.   Formulate bylaws for the advocacy group.

3.   Establish itself as a private nonprofit corporation in order to be eligible to receive funds from private sources and to attain a greater degree of autonomy from the appointing organizations.

4.   Recruit a juvenile justice task force to develop a more informed citizenry about the operation of the juvenile justice system and the persons this system seeks to serve, to provide needed political and economic support for the ACCY and to create a nucleus of persons who can make outstanding contributions as future members of the ACCY.

5.   Create job descriptions for the ACCY's technical staff and prepare the ACCY's annual operating budget.

SECURE FUNDING FROM PUBLIC AND PRIVATE SOURCES FOR THE POWER ADVOCACY GROUP.   The operation of the advocacy group should be financed by those organizations which appoint the advocacy group; however, state, federal and private funds should also be sought. Contributions from the general public and the juvenile justice task force can also be solicited. The influence of the juvenile justice task force should be fully utilized when requests for funding are made.

INITIATE OPERATION. The following procedures should be employed:

1. Recruit and select a technical staff which is highly qualified by training and experience to assist the ACCY to accomplish its objectives.

2. Appoint youth, parent, and professional advisory committees, and apprise them of their responsibilities.

3. Monitor progress the ACCY makes toward achieving its objectives and disseminate reports concerning this progress to the community and government.

In addition to using the foregoing procedures, the ACCY should fully utilize the resources of its technical staff, its youth, parent, and professional advisory committees, and its juvenile justice task force to augment its chances for success. In addition, the ACCY must not build up expectations for action faster than its capacity for action.

Operating Assumptions

When people have a difference of opinion about an issue, they are often operating on different sets of assumptions. To facilitate understanding of the power advocacy concept, the operating assumptions of power advocacy in juvenile justice are stated below.

1. The prevention and control of juvenile delinquency is an intense political process that involves who gets what, how, and when in terms of money, power, and service.

2. Local action is crucial to the success of juvenile justice advocacy because local officials are easily accessible to citizens, can be held accountable and, with sufficient community pressure, can be persuaded to expeditiously modify policies, programs, and

practices of local youth service organizations. Furthermore, elected local officials are in an excellent position to influence state and federal officials to employ delinquency prevention and control strategies desired by local communities.

3. Youth service personnel, although they be kind and dedicated, are first and foremost members of organizations where conflicts arise between the interests of youths and the organizations to which these persons are bureaucratically responsible.[1] Documented responses to youth by the juvenile court, public schools, and public social service agencies which are clearly designed to meet organizational needs rather than the needs of youth validate this assertion.

4. The technologies required to prevent and control juvenile delinquency are complex and not well developed. Consequently, cooperation among administrators of delinquency prevention and control services becomes very precarious because agency administrators, being committed to their agencies' imperfect techniques, are not inclined to cooperate with other agencies because of their concern that such cooperation, unless it is on their own terms, will threaten their autonomy and the wisdom of their approaches to delinquency prevention and/or control.[2]

5. Organizations, to succeed and survive, must adapt to the demands of their environments or those forces which influence organizational characteristics and outputs and which are potentially relevant to goal setting and attainment.[3] Consequently, in order to have the capability to significantly improve juvenile justice, residents of a locality must be able to exercise substantial control over the environments of the juvenile court and the network of youth service organizations with which the court interacts.

6. Although efforts to prevent delinquency have not been encouraging,[4] delinquency can be prevented, to some degree, if a locality is organized so as to possess the power to modify policies, programs, and practices of youth service organizations which contribute to youths being alienated and predisposed to committing delinquent acts. In this regard, it may be necessary for a locality to modify policies, programs, and practices which deny

youth access to educational and occupational roles and/or attach negative labels to youths which cause them to experience adjustment problems.

7. Juvenile delinquency can be controlled, to a significant extent, if residents of a locality are organized in a manner which enables them to persuade legislators and juvenile justice administrators to both define and administer certain forms of delinquent behavior (e.g., status offenses) out of existence,[5] and to effect the implementation of efficacious services for those youths who penetrate the juvenile justice system because they present a serious threat to persons or property.

8. Community-based delinquency prevention and control services which are locally identified and controlled will be more accountable, effective and economical than state administered delinquency prevention and control services.

The Need for Power Advocacy in Juvenile Justice

The Failure of Traditional Advocacy in Juvenile Justice

Advocacy, which involves a group or individual serving as a spokesman for another group or individual, is a frequently used strategy to improve juvenile justice. As many persons will testify, the amelioration of juvenile justice, for a number of reasons, constitutes a particularly arduous task. *(1)* The juvenile justice system has a pervasive statutory base which requires understanding of the law and legal expertise. *(2)* It is difficult to alter the responses of police to youths because police have a more rigid hierarchy than most organizations. *(3)* The enormous power and discretion of juvenile court judges creates significant obstacles to change. *(4)* There is a lack of demand for accountability in juvenile justice which is exemplified by the paucity of reviews of activities of the juvenile court by such regulatory agencies as the state supreme court, the dearth of monitoring of court services by state agencies, the marginal role of the prosecutor and defense attorney in the juvenile court and the lack of reliable and valid information about youth processed by the court. *(5)* Although only about 7% of the juvenile court cases involve serious crimes,[6] such as violent crimes against persons, many persons assume that many of the children and youths who become involved in the juvenile justice system are violent offenders deserving of punishment.

On the average, approximately 4% of the children and youths in a juvenile court jurisdiction will be processed annually.[7] Most of these youths have not committed violent crimes. Unfortunately, many youths who penetrate the juvenile justice system do not have the option of having people promote their special interests. In response to this situation, adults have formed advocacy groups to protect the legal and human rights of children and youths who become involved in the juvenile justice system, and to advocate for their futures. Some of the noble objectives which these advocacy groups have sought to accomplish include: *(1)* assessing efforts of public and private agencies to meet youth needs; *(2)* identifying and filling gaps in youth services; *(3)* coordinating, monitoring, and evaluating youth services; *(4)* disseminating information to the public about issues affecting troubled youths and their families; and *(5)* lobbying for legislation which serves the interests of youth.

Regretfully for youth and those persons who finance the operation of the juvenile court and other public and private youth service agencies, the afore described advocacy groups generally have not possessed sufficient power to effect significant changes in the juvenile court and the network of public and private agencies and organizations with which the court interacts. This paucity of power on behalf of juvenile justice advocacy groups is a major reason why these groups have failed to cause needed improvements in juvenile justice. Furthermore, these advocacy groups have not been inclined to accept the truism that change for youth is an intense political issue that involves who gets what, how, and when in terms of money, power, and service. The failure of juvenile justice advocacy groups to fully appreciate the political and economic ramifications related to modifying systems which serve youth is reflected in the membership of said groups. Typically, such groups have included representatives of youth service organizations (e.g., juvenile court, schools, welfare department, youth service bureau, etc.) who have an overriding interest in their organizations' survival. These persons, quite understandably, generally oppose policies or programs which might adversely affect their established interests. As a result, the debates about policies and programs related to the prevention and control of juvenile delinquency have frequently been less concerned with the substantive merits of said programs and policies than with the vested interests of organizations which advocacy group members represent. It is, therefore, not surprising that those successes experienced by juvenile justice advocacy groups have generally been restricted to identifying gaps in youth services and eliciting community support for the development of programs to fill these gaps, whereas the capacity of these groups to modify policies, programs, and practices of the juvenile court and other public and private youth service agencies has been minimal.

Isolation of the Juvenile Court

Findings of the National Assessment of Juvenile Corrections regarding the impact which the juvenile court's environment has on the court's operations were:

1. The influence of external organizations on the juvenile court is, at the most, limited.[8] Organizations which have the greatest influence on the courts are police, schools, state supreme courts, and the public prosecutor. These organizations are likely to pressure the court to maintain a law and order orientation. Organizations with the least influence on the court are civic and interest groups, private social services, and the public defender. These organizations tend to demand a social service orientation from the court.[9]

2. There is a pattern of low-level conflict between the juvenile court and the network of services with which it interacts. Furthermore, the influence of external organizations on the court is limited. There are a number of reasons why the juvenile court does

not have a demanding environment. *(1)* The courts generally do not make extensive use of resources in the environment, which prevents a dependence on any of these resources from developing. *(2)* The courts do not seem to make efforts to mobilize such resources or to challenge existing resources to serve youths in trouble, thus accounting for the low level of conflict with such agencies. *(3)* The relative insulation of the juvenile court from its environment may be a function of the overwhelming discretionary power vested in the hands of juvenile court judges. Having such discretionary power tends to limit the interaction of youth service agencies with courts because reciprocity is inhibited. Agencies which must deal with the court are likely to conform to its expectations and shy away from attempts to influence its policies. Other agencies, if possible, are likely to avoid any contact with the court.

    3.   There is little indication that courts actively pursue services in the community under their jurisdiction. In fact, on the average, courts rely four times as much on their own services as on those offered elsewhere; even though, court services typically involve only periodic monitoring of youths.[10]

    The consequences of these findings are that once youths enter the court's orbit, it is unlikely that the court will call upon other agencies for assistance or challenge their responses to adjudicated juveniles. Furthermore, there is no evidence to suggest that such agencies are willing to serve these youths. Rather, it seems they prefer the court to assume responsibility for them. Consequently, children and youths under court jurisdiction are likely to be thrust into a very narrow and limited pool of court services and be excluded from a wide variety of community youth services at a time when these services are most needed.[11]

Pressing Needs of Youth and the Juvenile Justice System Which Require Power Advocacy

    Following are some specific needs of youths and the juvenile justice system which power advocacy can address. These needs, which have been translated into *measurable* objectives, can be achieved in those localities which establish the power advocacy structure previously described. These objectives are listed under those organizations which have historically had the authority and opportunity to accomplish them, but which have generally failed to do so. It should be noted that *all* organizations under which objectives are listed may not have had the chance to achieve these objectives.

STATE LEGISLATURE, COUNTY GOVERNMENT, CITY GOVERNMENT, UNITED WAY, AND OTHER MAJOR SOURCES OF FUNDING FOR PRIVATE YOUTH SERVICE AGENCIES

1. To implement accountable diversion practices and programs for those youths who are not a serious threat to persons or property.

2. To improve the qualifications and, when justified, the emoluments of persons who deliver services designed to prevent and control delinquency, and to improve the quality and augment the quantity of pre-service and in-service training provided to these persons.

3. To increase accountability in juvenile justice by requiring those organizations which deliver delinquency control services to maintain appropriate information retrieval capacity, particularly about youths processed.

4. To ensure that the juvenile court and the organizations with whom they interact maintain cooperative interorganizational relationships.

5. To monitor and evaluate services on an ongoing basis in order to improve delinquency prevention and control service technologies and to make decisions regarding how the limited funds available for delinquency prevention and control programs might be expended most efficiently and effectively.

6. To modify policies, programs and practices of youth service organizations which deny youths access to meaningful educational and occupational roles and which attach negative labels to youths which create adjustment problems for them.

7. To create accountable and efficacious nonresidential and residential services which are most needed by youths who become involved in the juvenile justice system.

8. To expeditiously eliminate ineffective delinquency prevention and control services and to modify or merge delinquency prevention and control services when the need arises.

STATE LEGISLATURE, JUVENILE COURT, AND COUNTY GOVERNMENT

1. To deinstitutionalize those youths who are not a serious threat to persons or property.

2. To decrease the capacity of juvenile justice personnel, particularly judges, to intervene in the lives of so many youths on the basis of personal and professional belief systems, moral commitments, perceptions of community sentiment, and administrative convenience by eliminating from the jurisdiction of the court those offenses which would not be considered crimes if committed by an adult, and which do not present a threat to persons or property.

3. To improve the quality of defense counsel in the juvenile court and to provide due process protections at every stage of court proceedings, particularly intake, detention, adjudication, and disposition.

4. To improve the quality of the prosecutor in the juvenile court for the purposes of providing philosophical continuity concerning the role of the juvenile court and fairness to both youths and victims of youth crime.

5. To require the juvenile court to conduct regular reviews of children and youths in foster care for the following purposes:

   a. To reduce the large number of children and youths in foster care who are shuttled between foster homes and institutions without permanent plans for their care being formulated or implemented.

   b. To identify those youths who are drifting in foster care and/or who need to be given an opportunity to be adopted.

   c. To preclude youths in foster care from being removed

from foster homes and placed in new foster homes and institutions without notice.

d. To prevent youths from being returned to their original homes from foster care without court review.

6. To require the juvenile court to conduct regular reviews of youths who are placed on probation in order to:

a. Determine the quantity of counseling and casework services delivered by juvenile court personnel.

b. Ascertain community services to which youths have been referred and which have been utilized by them.

c. Identify positive and negative behaviors exhibited by youths since their previous probation review.

d. Modify conditions of probation which are ineffective and/or inappropriate.

STATE LEGISLATURE, COUNTY GOVERNMENT, AND STATE AGENCY RESPONSIBLE FOR JUVENILE CORRECTIONS.   To provide secure custody facilities with intensive, accountable treatment programs for those youths who present a serious threat to persons or property.

STATE LEGISLATURE, COUNTY GOVERNMENT, STATE AND COUNTY DEPARTMENTS OF SOCIAL SERVICES.   To increase the quantity and quality of protective services for children and youths who are in a condition of neglect and dependency for the purposes of augmenting the chances these youth will remain in their own homes or return from foster care at the earliest possible date.

STATE SUPREME COURT.   To monitor the juvenile court's compliance with mandated due process requirements.

STATE AGENCY RESPONSIBLE FOR JUVENILE CORRECTIONS, STATE AND COUNTY DEPARTMENTS OF SOCIAL SERVICES, LOCAL SCHOOL BOARD, AND COUNTY GOVERNMENT.   To reduce the use of behavior modifying drugs in institutions and schools, eliminate the overuse of corporal punishment in child care institutions, foster homes, and schools and to demand that institutions refrain from depriving youths of meals, mail, and visits by their families, and exposing youths to solitary confinement, sexual abuse, and discipline by peers.

STATE LEGISLATURE, COUNTY GOVERNMENT, AND CITY GOVERNMENT. To ensure that local and state governments are not spending more money for social control of nondangerous juvenile offenders than they are spending for positive socialization through appropriate educational, social, psychological, medical, recreational, and employment services.

FOUR REASONS FOR THE EFFICACY OF POWER ADVOCACY IN JUVENILE JUSTICE

Power advocacy will result in ameliorated juvenile justice for a number of reasons: *(1)* power advocacy in juvenile justice will influence changes in policies, programs, and practices of the juvenile court and the organizations with which the court has transactions because it will be able to control, to a significant degree, the external environments of these organizations; *(2)* the need for power advocacy in juvenile justice is so evident and easily documented that many persons will be persuaded that it should be utilized to prevent and control juvenile delinquency; *(3)* power advocacy will be attractive to numerous groups in the community because these groups will perceive that they will benefit from its implementation; and *(4)* the impact of power advocacy can be measured.

The Environments of the Juvenile Court and the Network of Agencies with which it Interacts are Vulnerable to Power Advocacy

Juvenile courts are dynamic and open systems characterized by a complex set of relations and transactions with various external organizations and units in their immediate environment. These relations are established because the court needs external resources and services and because these external units need the services of the court. Agencies and organizations with which the court transacts in order to fulfill its mission include:[12]

1.   Agencies that refer youths to the court, such as police, schools, and social service agencies.

2.   Organizations that provide fiscal resources to the court, such as county government, state department of social services, state youth service departments.

3.   Organizations that monitor and evaluate the operation of the court, such as the state supreme court, public prosecutor, and public defender.

4.   Organizations that provide complementary services, such as psychological and medical services, public and private child service agencies, and youth service bureaus.

5.   Organizations that receive court referrals, such as state youth service agencies, child welfare agency, probation, and detention departments.

6.   Organizations with general interest and concern in the court, such as child advocacy groups, and civic clubs.

As has been documented earlier, juvenile courts experience minimal dependence on the agencies and organizations with which they interact; however, they must maintain systematic relationships with some of these agencies to assure a steady flow of services.

The fact that the juvenile court does not currently face a demanding environment does not change the validity of the proposition that organizations, in order to succeed and survive, will modify their goals in accordance with the demands of their environments.[13] The introduction of power advocacy in juvenile justice will create a much more demanding environment for the juvenile court and youth service organizations with which it has transactions because a locality's Advocacy Commission for Children and Youth will be authorized by organizations on which these youth service organizations are most dependent for funding to perform the following tasks:

1.   Recommend the elimination, modification, merger, ex-

pansion and/or creation of delinquency prevention and control policies, programs, and practices.

2. To, on an ongoing basis, monitor and evaluate all delinquency prevention and control programs.

3. To investigate *all* problems relating to the delivery of youth services and to recommend actions to remediate those problems identified.

4. To engage in litigation to rectify abuses of systems that serve youths.

The impact of a locality's ACCY on the environments of all youth service organizations, especially the juvenile court and other youth service organizations which provide delinquency prevention and control services, will be significant because the ACCY will have the capability to place environmental constraints and contingencies on *all* youth service organizations. Youth service organizations, particularly the juvenile court, are sensitive to political undercurrents and attempt to avoid controversy. An ACCY, which certainly can create political undercurrents and controversy in regard to the performances of youth service organizations, will have the ability to alter the responses of these organizations because these organizations will find it necessary to manage relations with their environments in order to preserve and maintain themselves, to secure stable resources, to achieve their goals, to be perceived as fit for future action and to survive. It seems evident that the environments of all youth service organizations in a locality served by a juvenile court will, to varying degrees, be vulnerable to power advocacy. This means that the ACCY will have the necessary influence to make these organizations more responsive, accountable, efficient, and effective.

A Locality Will Perceive the Need for Power Advocacy in Juvenile Justice

It is clear that many people have become alarmed about juvenile crime, especially serious crimes against persons or property. People want juvenile crime prevented and controlled to a greater extent than is currently being accomplished. Persons become distressed and concerned when they find that a majority of youths who become involved in the juvenile justice system do not penetrate this system because they have committed a violent crime, but because they are a status offender or have engaged in petty delinquent acts.[14] Persons become even more upset when they learn that status offenders and youth who commit petty delinquent acts are less likely to be afforded due process protections, and more likely to be incarcerated in correctional institutions, than juveniles who commit serious delinquent offenses.[15] People become further agitated when they are apprised that less than one-half of juvenile probation officers have had professional training in criminal justice, corrections, or social work,[16] and that youths caught in the net of the juvenile court are unlikely to receive needed services because the court is unwilling to challenge community agencies to deliver these services, and public and private youth service agencies resist serving clients of the juvenile court. Finally, people become both sad and angry when they are informed that about one-third of the dependent and neglected youths which the juvenile court places in foster care drift from one foster home and institution to another without a permanent plan for their care being formulated or implemented. Power advocacy in juvenile justice will be supported by local communities because its need is glaring, and, to put it mildly, a substantial number of people are no longer willing to stand by quietly and allow the responsibility for a community's failure to prevent and control juvenile delinquency to be lost in the bureaucracy of the juvenile justice system, or lost in the proposition that failure is imbedded in our children and youth.

Influential Local Groups and Organizations will Determine that they will Derive Benefits from the Implementation of Power Advocacy in Juvenile Justice

The implementation of power advocacy in juvenile justice will not occur just because it is direly needed. Key groups and organizations in a locality served by a juvenile court must be convinced that they will benefit in some way through the use of power advocacy. Those groups and organizations in a locality serviced by a juvenile court which will determine that they will derive benefits from the use of power advocacy in juvenile justice include:

1. *Local Groups on Which Youth Service Organizations are Most Dependent for Financial Resources.* Public and private funding sources will become aware of all youth services available in a locality served by a juvenile court and the annual cost of these services. They will be informed, on an ongoing basis, about the efficacy of delinquency prevention and control services which they finance, will have the capability to investigate and remediate all youth service delivery problems expeditiously, and will have the ability to eliminate, modify, merge, expand, and/or create delinquency prevention and control policies, programs, and practices. Finally, both public and private funding sources will be viewed by youth service professionals, youths, parents, and religions, service, and civic organizations and the general public as expending public and private funds for only those delinquency prevention and control programs which have a measurable impact on preventing and controlling juvenile delinquency and improving juvenile justice.

2. *Youth Service Organizations.* Youth service personnel will have more services available for their clients and will, through representation on the ACCY's professional advisory committee, have an opportunity to critically evaluate proposals to eliminate, modify, merge, expand, and/or create delinquency prevention and control policies, programs, and practices. They will also be able to use the ACCY to both investigate problems relating to the effective delivery of youth services and to remediate those problems identified.

3. *Parents.* Parents will have more effective services available for both their children and themselves. Through representation on the ACCY's parent advisory committee, parents will be able to critically evaluate proposals to eliminate, merge, modify, expand, and/or create delinquency prevention and control poli-

cies, programs, and practices. They will have an opportunity to report problems relating to youth service delivery to the ACCY for investigation and remediation.

4. *Children and Youths.* Children and youths will have access to needed services. Through representation on the ACCY's youth advisory committee, youths will be able to critically evaluate proposals to eliminate, merge, modify, expand, and/or create delinquency prevention and control policies, programs, and practices. They will also be able to report problems relating to youth service delivery to the ACCY for investigation and remediation.

5. *Religious, Service, and Civic Organizations.* Through their participation on the ACCY's juvenile justice task force, representatives of these organizations will have the opportunity to play a significant role in preventing and controlling juvenile delinquency by supporting, politically and economically, implementation of recommendations made by the ACCY. They will also have a chance to prepare themselves to serve on the ACCY.

The Impact of Power Advocacy in Juvenile Justice can be Measured

The success and effectiveness of the Advocacy Commission for Children and Youth, or any organization for that matter, should be judged by the degree to which it achieves its objectives. The need for power advocacy in juvenile justice has been previously identified and translated into measurable objectives. It is suggested that the following indicators might be utilized to measure the efficacy of power advocacy in juvenile justice in a locality served by a juvenile court.

INDICATORS OF PROGRESS MADE TOWARD PREVENTING JUVENILE DELINQUENCY

1. A reduction in the number of children and youths drifting in foster care without permanent plans for their care being formulated or implemented.

2. An increase in the number of youths drifting in foster

care who are given a legal status which enables them to be adopted.

3. An increase in the number of youths in foster care whose cases are reviewed on a regular basis.

4. Documented improvement in the quantity and quality of protective services delivered to dependent and neglected children and youths.

5. A decrease in school truancy, school suspensions, school expulsions, and school dropouts.

Indicators of Advancement Made Toward Controlling Juvenile Delinquency

1. An increase in the number of probation reviews conducted by the juvenile court.

2. A decrease in the rate of self-reported delinquency.

3. A reduction in the number of youths processed by the juvenile justice system as shown by the number of arrests of juveniles, referrals to the juvenile court, petitions filed alleging the commission of status offenses, or misdemeanor offenses or felony offenses, adjudication hearings, youths who are waived to adult court, youths who are incarcerated in detention centers, jails and juvenile correctional institutions, and the length of time youths are required to remain in these facilities.

4. A reduction in court counselor caseloads and recidivism rates of youths who have disposition hearings.

5. An increase in the availability of accountable, secure custody, intensive treatment programs for youths who present a serious threat to persons or property.

Indicators of Progress Made Toward Improving the Delivery of Juvenile Justice

1. Increased "activity" of defense attorneys and prosecutors in juvenile court.

2. Documented changes in policies, programs, and practices of the juvenile court and other youth service organizations

which occurred as a result of recommendations made by the ACCY.

3. Documented examples of improved cooperation between the juvenile court and the network of agencies with which it interacts.

4. Documented improvements in the capability of the juvenile court and other organizations which provide delinquency prevention and control services to maintain appropriate information retrieval capacity about children and youths they process.

5. A decrease in the use of behavior modifying drugs in child care institutions and schools.

6. A reduction in the use of corporal punishment in child care institutions, foster homes, and schools.

7. An increase in the number of youths in institutions who are able to receive mail and be visited by their families.

8. A reduction in the number of youths in institutions who are placed in solitary confinement and exposed to sexual abuse and discipline by peers.

9. An increase in the number of delinquency prevention and control services which are monitored and evaluated.

10. The number of delinquency prevention and control services which are eliminated, modified, merged, expanded, or created as a result of recommendations by the ACCY.

11. The number of problems related to the delivery of youth services reported to the ACCY which are investigated, identified, and remediated.

12. The number of court actions which are initiated to rectify abuses in systems which serve youths.

13. An increase in the number of youths who have an attorney at every stage of juvenile court proceedings.

14. An increase in the number of appeals of juvenile cases.

15. An increase in the number of youths who, through policies, programs, and practices of delinquency prevention and control agencies, are either diverted from the juvenile court or deinstitutionalized.

Regardless which of the foregoing indicators are used to

measure the impact of power advocacy in juvenile justice, baseline data for each of these indicators must be obtained. In a number of instances, such baseline data may not be available. If such data are available, the ACCY will have the power required to obtain it.

IMPLICATIONS OF POWER ADVOCACY IN JUVENILE JUSTICE FOR STATE YOUTH SERVICE BUREAUCRACIES

Because of increasing costs, the fiscal burden and responsibility for the operation and oversight of juvenile corrections programs have shifted steadily from local to state governments.[17] As a result, massive state youth service bureaucracies have been created which require large expenditures of tax dollars to, primarily, finance the operation of ineffective, inhumane, and expensive juvenile correctional institutions, frequently termed "warehouses for youth." In a national study of juvenile corrections in the United States, Downs, Hall, and Vinter determined that only four of 48 reporting states assigned as many youths to community correction programs as to institutional settings; even though, community correction programs are more economical and at least as effective as institutions. States which utilized community corrections programs frequently used them to expand the juvenile justice system rather than to serve as substitutes for institutions.[18] Hasenfeld and Sarri found that state administered juvenile probation services provided no greater consistency and effectiveness than did probation services operated under local auspices.[19]

It has been asserted that power advocacy in juvenile justice, if implemented properly, can effect significant improvements in juvenile justice, particularly at the local level where juvenile court judges, with their almost unrestrained power, determine what juvenile justice in localities served by their courts will be like. Power advocacy must also be used to eliminate and modify aspects of state youth service bureaucracies which neither serve the interests of youth nor taxpayers. It is suggested that this objective might be best accomplished by a number of local ACCYs joining together for the purpose of creating a political force with sufficient strength to expeditiously alter policies, programs, and practices of state youth service bureaucracies. Since each ACCY, because of its affiliation with local elected officials, will have political clout at the state level, it seems that an organization of ACCYs would possess enormous political influence.

There are strategies which an influential ACCY, or an organization of numerous ACCYs might use to both substantially reduce the size of a state youth service bureaucracy and secure funds to implement locally identified and controlled delinquency prevention and control services. One strongly recommended strategy would be to demand that a high percentage of funds appropriated by a state legislature to finance delinquency prevention and control services be disbursed to local units of government to be used for delinquency prevention and control efforts recommended by a locality's ACCY. It is obvious this strategy would have tremendous implications for a state youth service bureaucracy because it would mean that state agencies would begin to play a less important role in the delivery of delinquency prevention and control services. Instead, this responsibility would be assumed by local units of government which would utilize the resources of an ACCY to make decisions with regard to how state, local, and private delinquency prevention and control funds were expended.

A FINAL COMMENT

As has been elucidated, power advocacy can effect significant improvements in juvenile justice at both the state and local levels. Without power advocacy, juvenile court judges, and other politicians who are inclined to pose as juvenile justice experts, will continue to hold the power necessary to negate efforts of concerned individuals and groups who seek to ameliorate juvenile justice. Although power advocacy is not a panacea, it is a sound approach which can be used to both deal with obstacles to change and to improve a complex social institution which has been resistant to meaningful change for far too long.

Chapter 8

RECOMMENDATIONS FOR THE JUVE-
NILE COURT AND ORGANIZATIONS
AND AGENCIES WITH WHICH THE
COURT INTERACTS

The authors believe that in order for a state to make substantial progress toward the improvement of juvenile justice and the prevention and control of juvenile delinquency, its juvenile courts and agencies and organizations with which these courts interact must implement the recommendations specified below. Rationales for these recommendations are elucidated in the foregoing chapters.

POLICE

1.   Formulate and implement written policies and procedures designed to create effective working relationships with the juvenile court, public schools, youth service agencies, and the community (see Chapters 4 and 5).

2.   Provide police officers with specialized training designed to prepare them to respond appropriately to juvenile crime and youth problems (see Chapters 4 and 5).

3. Expand police diversion programs and administer these programs in a manner which: (a) places greater accountability on parents and youth service agencies for developing and delivering services needed by problem youth; and (b) results in a significant reduction in the number of youths referred to juvenile court intake by police (see Chapter 4).

4. Police agencies should establish written policies and guidelines to support police discretionary authority, at the point of first contact as well as at the police station, to divert juveniles to alternative community-based programs and human resource agencies outside the juvenile justice system, when the safety of the community is not jeopardized. Disposition may include: (a) release on the basis of unfounded charges; (b) referral to parents (warning and release); (c) referral to social agencies; and (d) referral to juvenile court intake services. Police should not have discretionary authority to make detention decisions. This responsibility must rest with the court, which should assume control over admissions on a 24-hour basis (see Chapter 4).

5. Refer to juvenile court intake only those youths who have committed more than two offenses against persons or property, or who have committed less than two such offenses, and who present an imminent threat to other persons or property (see Chapter 4).

JUVENILE COURT

1. Allocate more human and economic resources to youths who have committed offenses against persons or property (see Chapters 1–5).

2. Discontinue processing youths who have only committed a status offense(s) (see Chapters 3 and 4).

3. Desist seeking to maintain control over services to which the court refers youths or to administer youth services which can be delivered effectively by agencies outside the juvenile justice system (see Chapter 4).

4. Institute restitution programs for victims of youth crime (see Chapters 4 and 5).

5. Promote the development of a juvenile justice information system which will provide juvenile justice officials with the management information they require to improve the effectiveness and efficiency of the juvenile justice system (see Chapter 4).

6. Provide youths access to counsel at all stages of juvenile court proceedings (see Chapters 2 and 6).

7. Detain in a juvenile detention center *only* those youths who present a serious threat to other persons or property, and who are unlikely to appear at their court hearing unless they are detained (see Chapters 2 and 5).

8. Incarcerate in juvenile correctional institutions only those youths who present a serious threat to other persons or property (see Chapters 1 and 5).

9. Review, on a regular basis, the status of all youths placed in the custody of public social service agencies (see Chapters 3 and 7).

10. Review, on a regular basis, the progress of all youths placed on probation (see Chapters 2 and 7).

11. Require juvenile intake officers to employ the practice of "true diversion" (see Chapter 4).

12. Support the implementation of power advocacy in juvenile justice (see Chapter 7).

Public Schools

1. Provide or contract for intensive counseling and casework services for all youth under the jurisdiction of the juvenile court who are chronic truants and/or who exhibit behavior problems in the school setting on a regular basis. These services should be delivered on a frequent basis in home and school settings at times convenient for those youth and parents being served (see Chapters 3, 4, and 7).

2. Provide or contract for competency based academic, social, vocational and physical skill development programs for all youths under the jurisdiction of the juvenile court who have demonstrated deficiencies in one or more of these areas. Priority should be given to those youths who are chronic truants and/or who exhibit behavior problems at school on a regular basis and/or who are involved with the juvenile court because of their commission of a delinquent act(s) (see Chapters 3, 4, and 7).

3. Provide or contract for in-school suspension programs for all youths within the age jurisdiction of the juvenile court who require these services (see Chapters 3, 4, and 7).

4. Refer to juvenile court intake only those youths who have committed an act which would be considered a crime if committed by an adult (see Chapters 3 and 4).

PUBLIC SOCIAL SERVICE AGENCIES

1. Provide or contract for the delivery of high quality protective services for youths who are reported to the agency as being without the care necessary for his/her physical, mental, or emotional health, or who are abandoned, or who are physically, mentally, or emotionally abused, or neglected or sexually abused (see Chapter 3).

2. Provide or contract for high quality foster care services for youth in the agency's custody. These services should include, but are not limited to: (a) group home treatment units; (b) specialized foster care; and (c) temporary shelter care (see Chapters 3–5).

3. Develop strategies to effect the adoption of those youths who are destined to remain in foster care for a long period of time, and who are unlikely to be returned to their natural parents (see Chapters 3 and 7).

4. Terminate the practice of filing juvenile petitions against youths who run away from foster care, unless said youths have committed an act which would be considered a crime if committed by an adult (see Chapters 3 and 4).

Private Youth Service Agencies

Modify policies, programs, and practices which preclude problem youths from gaining access to private youth services. Such modification may include; (a) making services available to youths at times and places convenient for those being served; (b) offering services at no charge to clients; (c) developing and delivering services most needed by problem youths; and (d) changing aspects of programs which do not meet the needs of certain problem youth, rather than rejecting these youth from these programs (see Chapters 3 and 4).

Youth Advocates

Implement power advocacy in juvenile justice (see Chapter 7).

Local Government

Encourage and support the implementation of power advocacy in juvenile justice (see Chapter 7).

State Legislature

1. Eliminate status offenses from the jurisdiction of the juvenile court (see Chapters 1 and 3).
2. Deinstitutionalize all those youths who do not present a serious threat to other persons or property (see Chapters 1 and 5).
3. Phase out all youth juvenile correctional institutions which have a capacity to handle over 200 youths at one time (see Chapters 1 and 5).
4. Allocate block grants of state funds to local units of government which employ power advocacy in juvenile justice in

order that localities can develop community-based correctional programs for juvenile offenders (see Chapter 7).

5.   Increase qualifications and emoluments for all juvenile justice officials, particularly those officials who have the greatest amount of interaction with youth who penetrate the juvenile justice system (see Chapters 2 and 7).

6.   Allocate sufficient funds to state juvenile correctional agencies to finance the operation of small secure custody facilities where high quality treatment programs are provided for those youths who are chronic offenders and who present a serious threat to other persons or property (see Chapters 1, 5, and 7).

STATE SUPREME COURT

1.   Monitor the activities of juvenile courts more closely (see Chapter 6).

2.   Encourage law schools to offer specialized training programs for persons interested in serving as judges, prosecutors, and defense counsel in the juvenile and family courts (see Chapter 6).

NOTES

CHAPTER 1

1. Abbott, Grace. *The Child and the State*, Vol. II. Chicago: University of Chicago Press, 1938, p. 343.

2. Thurston, Henry W. *The Dependent Child: A Story of Changing Aims and Methods in the Care of Dependent Children*. New York: Columbia University Press, 1930, p. 90.

3. Abbott. op. cit., pp. 392–400.

4. Kobrin, Solomon. "The Chicago Area Project—a 25-Year Assessment." *The Annals of the American Academy of Political and Social Science.* (March, 1959), pp. 27–28.

5. Sandhu, Harjit S. *Modern Corrections, The Offenders, Therapies and Community Reintegration*. Springfield, Illinois: Charles C Thomas, 1974, pp. 14–20.

6. Sandhu, Harjit S. *Juvenile Delinquency: Causes, Control, and Prevention*. New York: McGraw-Hill Book Company, 1977, pp. 34–42.

7. Wadsworth, Benjamin. *The Well-ordered Family or Relative Duties*. (Boston, 1712), pp. 44–59, 90–102; cited in David Rothman *The Discovery of the Asylum*. Boston: Little Brown, 1971, p. 16.

8. Rothman. op. cit., p. 213.

9. Lathrop, Julia. "The Development of the Probation System in a Large City." *Charities, 13* (January, 1905): 348; cited in Anthony M. Platt *The Child Savers,* 2nd ed. Chicago: University of Chicago Press, 1969, 1977, p. 36.

10. Platt, Anthony M. *The Child Savers, the Invention of Delinquency* (2nd ed.). Chicago: University of Chicago Press, 1977, p. 3.

11. Ibid., p. 4.

12. Ibid., p. 75.

13. Ibid., p. 99.

14. Ibid., p. 134.

15. Ibid., p. xxi.

16. deMause, Lloyd. "The Nightmare of Childhood," in Beatrice Gross and Ronald Gross (eds.), *The Children's Rights Movement.* Garden City, New York: Anchor Books, 1977, pp. 33–35.

17. Ibid., p. 35.

18. Steinmetz, S. K. & Straus, Murray A. "The Family as Cradle of Violence." *Society, 10* (6), 1973, 50–56.

19. Gil, David G. *Violence Against Children: Physical Child Abuse in the United States.* Cambridge, Mass.: Harvard University Press, 1970, p. 108.

20. Hartjen, Clayton A. *Crime and Criminalization* (2nd ed.). New York: Holt, Rinehart & Winston/Praeger, 1978, p. 14.

21. National Association of Counties Research Foundation, *Juvenile Delinquency: A Basic Manual for County Officials.* Washington: National Association of Counties Research Foundation, 1976, p. 2.

22. Figlio, Robert M., Sellin, Thorsten, & Wolfgang, Marvin E. *Delinquency in a Birth Cohort.* Chicago: University of Chicago Press, 1972, p. 251.

23. Hasenfeld, Y. & Sarri, R. (eds.) *Brought to Justice? Juveniles, the Court and the Law.* Ann Arbor, Mich.: National Assessment of Juvenile Corrections, University of Michigan, 1976, p. 198.

CHAPTER 2

1. President's Commission on Law Enforcement and Administration of Justice. *The Challenge of Crime in a Free Society.* Washington: U.S. Government Printing Office, 1967, p. 78.

2. Kobetz, R. W. & Bosarge, Betty. *Juvenile Justice Administration*. Gaithersburg, Maryland: International Association of Chiefs of Police, 1973, p. 132.

3. Ibid., p. 139.

4. Ibid., p. 155.

5. President's Commission on Law Enforcement and Administration of Justice. *The Challenge of Crime in a Free Society*, op. cit., p. 82.

6. National Advisory Commission on Criminal Justice Standards and Goals. *Corrections*. Washington: U.S. Government Printing Office, 1973, p. 264.

7. Kobetz, Richard W. *The Police Role and Juvenile Delinquency*. Gaithersburg, Maryland: International Association of Chiefs of Police, 1971, p. 118.

8. Kobetz & Bosarge. *Juvenile Justice Administration*, op. cit., p. 141.

9. Piersma, Paul et al. *Law and Tactics in Juvenile Law*. Philadelphia, Pa.: American Law Institute-American Bar Association, 1977, p. 4.

10. Ibid., pp. 4–5.

11. Finestone, Harold. *Victims of Change*. Westport, Conn.: Greenwood Press, 1971, p. 41.

12. Platt, Anthony M. *The Child Savers*. Chicago: University of Chicago Press, 1969, p. 152.

13. Healy, William & Bronner, Augusta F. *Delinquents and Criminals: Their Making and Unmaking*. New York: Macmillan Company, 1926, p. 201.

14. Shaw, Clifford D. & McKay, Henry D. *Juvenile Delinquency and Urban Areas*. Chicago: University of Chicago Press, 1942, pp. 182–183.

15. U.S. Department of Justice, Law Enforcement Assistance Administration. *Juvenile Court Statistics*. Washington: National Institute for Juvenile Justice and Delinquency Prevention, 1974, p. 6.

16. Vinter, Robert D. "The Juvenile Court as an Institution." Appendix C in the President's Commission on Law Enforcement and Administration of Justice, *Task Force Report: Juvenile Delinquency and Youth Crime*, Washington, U.S. Government Printing Office, 1967.

17. Ibid., pp. 84–85.

18. Ibid., p. 85.

19. Ibid., p. 88.

20. Lemert, Edwin M. "The Juvenile Court—Quest and Realities." Appendix D in the President's Commission on Law Enforcement, *Task Force Report: Juvenile Delinquency*, op. cit., p. 92.

21. Murphy, Patrick T. *Our Kindly Parent . . . The State*. New York: Viking, pp. 8–9.

22. President's Commission on Law Enforcement and Administration of Justice. *Task Force Report, Juvenile Delinquency and Youth Crime*. op. cit., p. 94.

23. Ibid., p. 3.

24. Kent vs. United States. *United States Reports*, Vol. 383, 1966, pp. 541–565.

25. Ibid., p. 551.

26. Ibid., pp. 553–554.

27. Ibid., pp. 555–556.

28. *United States Reports*, Vol. 387, pp. 1–81.

29. Ibid., p. 21.

30. Ibid., p. 16.

31. Ibid., p. 26.

32. Sarri, Rosemary C. *Under Lock and Key: Juveniles in Jails and Detention*. National Assessment of Juvenile Corrections. Ann Arbor, Mich.: University of Michigan, December 1974.

33. U.S. Department of Justice, Law Enforcement Assistance Administration, National Criminal Justice Information and Statistics Service. *National Jail Census, 1970: A Report on the Nation's Local Jails and Types of Inmates*. Washington: U.S. Government Printing Office, 1971.

34. Sarri, R. C. op. cit., pp. 5–6.

35. Ibid., p. 9.

36. Ibid., p. 10.

37. Ibid., p. 12.

38. Ibid., p. 17.

39. Ibid., pp. 64–65.

40. Ibid., p. 65.

41. Ibid., p. 29.

42. Ibid., p. 30.

43. Ibid., pp. 17–19.

44. Haarman, G. B. & Sandefur, B. *Analysis of Detention*. Louisville and Jefferson County, Kentucky: Metropolitan Social Service Department, 1972, cited in Sarri, *Under Lock and Key*, op. cit., p. 32.

45. U.S. Department of Justice, Law Enforcement Assistance Administration,

Children in Custody (1973). Washington: National Criminal Justice Information and Statistics Service, December, 1977, p. 19.

46. Sarri. *Under Lock and Key.* op. cit., p. 62.

CHAPTER 3

1. Sarri, Rosemary C. *Remarks Presented at the Hearings of the House of Representatives Select Committee on Crime.* The National Assessment of Juvenile Corrections. Ann Arbor, Mich.: University of Michigan, 1973, pp. 6–9.

2. Task Force on Juvenile Delinquency, The President's Crime Commission on Law Enforcement and Administration of Justice. *Juvenile Delinquency and Youth Crime.* Washington: U.S. Government Printing Office, 1967, p. 27.

3. National Council of Crime and Delinquency. "Jurisdiction Over Status Offenses Should be Removed From the Juvenile Court." *Crime and Delinquency* (April, 1975), p. 97.

4. National Association of Counties. *Juvenile Justice and Delinquency Prevention Platform.* Washington: National Association of Counties, 1976, p. 1.

5. Hasenfeld, Y. & Sarri, R. (eds.). *Brought to Justice? Juveniles, the Courts and the Law.* Ann Arbor, Mich.: National Assessment of Juvenile Corrections, University of Michigan, 1976, p. 71.

6. *Crime and Delinquency* (April, 1975), op. cit., p. 97.

7. Davis, Samuel M. *Rights of Juveniles: The Juvenile Justice System.* New York: Clark Boardman Company, Ltd., 1974, p. 20.

8. Hasenfeld, op. cit., p. 217.

9. Stumphauzer, Jerome S. (ed.). *Behavior Therapy With Delinquents.* Springfield, Illinois: Charles C Thomas, 1973, p. 24.

10. National Association of Counties Research Foundation. *Juvenile Delinquency: A Basic Manual for County Officials.* Washington: National Association of Counties Research Foundation, 1976, p. 3.

11. Hasenfeld, op. cit., p. 217.

12. Figlio, Robert M., Sellin, Thorsten & Wolfgang, Marvin E. *Delinquency in a Birth Cohort.* Chicago: University of Chicago Press, 1972, p. 252.

13. Hasenfeld. op. cit., p. 213.

14. Ibid.

15. Ibid., p. 213.

16. Dixon, Michael C. and William E. Wright, *Juvenile Delinquency Prevention Programs: An Evaluation of Policy Related Research on the Effectiveness of Prevention Programs: Report on the Findings of an Evaluation of the Literature.* Nashville: Peabody College for Teachers, 1975, p. 18–20.

17. Figlio et al. op. cit., p. 5.

18. Hasenfeld. op. cit., p. 213.

19. *Crime and Delinquency* (April, 1975). op. cit., p. 98.

20. Gold, Martin and Jay R. Williams, "National Study of the Aftermath of Apprehension," *Prospectus,* December, 1969, p. 4.

21. Vinter, Robert D. (ed.). *Time Out: A National Study of Juvenile Correctional Problems.* Ann Arbor, Mich.: National Assessment of Juvenile Corrections, University of Michigan, 1976, pp. 183–184.

22. Hasenfeld. op. cit., p. 71.

23. Figlio et al. op. cit., p. 245.

24. Ferdinand, Theodore and Elmer G. Luchterhand, "Inner City Youth, the Police, the Juvenile Court and Justice." *Social Problems,* 1970, Vol. 17, p. 510.

25. Sarri, Rosemary C. *Under Lock and Key: Juveniles in Jail and Detention.* Ann Arbor, Mich,: National Assessment of Juvenile Corrections, University of Michigan, 1974, p. 65.

26. U.S. Department of Justice. *Program Announcement: Diversion of Youth From the Juvenile Justice System.* op. cit., p. 17.

27. Sarri. op. cit., p. 65.

28. Thomas, Charles S. "Are Status Offenders Really so Different?" *Crime and Delinquency* (October, 1976), p. 438.

29. Clarke, Stevens H. "Letter to the Editor." *Crime and Delinquency* (July 1977), pp. 333–334.

30. Figlio et al. op. cit., p. 252.

31. Davis. op. cit., p. 47.

32. *Crime and Delinquency* (April, 1975). op. cit., p. 98.

CHAPTER 4

1. U.S. Department of Health, Education and Welfare, Social and Rehabilitation Service. *The Challenge of Youth Service Bureaus.* Washington: U.S. Government Printing Office, 1973, p. 15.

2. Nejelski, Paul. "Diversion: The Promise and Danger." *Crime and Delinquency* (October, 1976), p. 393.

3. Klein, Malcolm W. "Issues and Realities in Police Diversion Programs." *Crime and Delinquency* (October, 1976), p. 421.

4. McDermott, R. & Rutherford, Andrew. *Juvenile Diversion*. Washington: U.S. Government Printing Office, 1976, p. 3.

5. U.S. Department of Justice, Office of Juvenile Justice and Delinquency Prevention. *Program Announcement: Diversion of Youth From the Juvenile Justice System*. Washington: U.S. Law Enforcement Assistance Administration, 1976, p. 101.

6. Ibid., p. 8.

7. Sarri, R. "Diversion—Within and Without the Juvenile Justice System." *Soundings on Youth*. Tucson, Arizona: National Council on Crime and Delinquency, March-April, 1975, pp. 11–12.

8. Kobetz, R. & Bosarge, Betty. *Juvenile Justice Administration*. Gaithersburg, Maryland: International Association of Police Chiefs, Inc., 1973, p. 70.

9. Downs, George, Hall, John & Vinter, Robert D. *Juvenile Corrections in the States: Residential Programs and Deinstitutionalization*. Ann Arbor, Mich.: National Assessment of Juvenile Corrections, University of Michigan, 1976, pp. 48–49.

10. McDermott. op. cit., p. 26.

11. Cressey, D. R. & McDermott, R. *Diversion From the Juvenile Justice System*. Ann Arbor, Mich.: National Assessment of Juvenile Corrections, the University of Michigan, 1973, p. 6.

12. McDermott. op. cit., p. 26.

13. Ibid., p. 26.

14. Ibid., pp. 27–38.

15. Task Force on Juvenile Delinquency, The President's Crime Commission on Law Enforcement and the Administration of Justice. *Juvenile Delinquency and Youth Crime*. Washington: U.S. Government Printing Office, 1967, p. 2.

16. Kobetz. op. cit., pp. 4–5.

17. Ibid., p. 73.

18. National Advisory Commission on Criminal Justice Standards and Goals. *Community Crime Prevention*. Washington: U.S. Government Printing Office, 1973, p. 70.

19. National Council on Crime and Delinquency. "Jurisdiction Over Status

Offenses Should be Removed From the Juvenile Court." *Crime and Delinquency* (April, 1975), p. 97.

20. National Association of Counties. *Juvenile Justice and Delinquency Prevention Platform*. Washington: National Association of Counties, 1976, p. 1.

21. Office of Juvenile Justice and Delinquency Prevention. op. cit., p. 101.

22. U.S. Department of Justice, Office of Juvenile Justice and Delinquency Prevention. *First Comprehensive Plan for Federal Juvenile Delinquency Programs*. Washington: Law Enforcement Assistance Administration, 1976, p. 9.

23. Cressey. op. cit., p. 2.

24. Shur, Edwin M. *Radical Nonintervention: Rethinking the Delinquency Problem*. Englewood Cliffs, New Jersey: Prentice-Hall, Inc., 1973, pp. 121–125.

25. Lemert, Edwin M. *Instead of Court: Diversion in Juvenile Justice*. Washington: U.S. Government Printing Office, 1971.

25a. Ibid., pp. 11–12.

26. Shur. op. cit., p. 126.

27. Ibid., p. 164.

28. Cressey. op. cit., p. 2.

29. Stumphauzer, Jerome S. (ed.). *Behavior Therapy With Delinquents*. Springfield, Illinois: Charles C Thomas, 1973, pp. 83–84.

30. McDermott. op. cit., p. 4.

31. Hasenfeld, Y. & Sarri, R. (eds.). *Brought to Justice? Juveniles, the Courts and the Law*. Ann Arbor, Mich.: National Assessment of Juvenile Corrections, University of Michigan, 1976, p. 217.

32. Ibid., p. 95.

33. Ibid., p. 153.

34. Ibid., p. 213.

35. Lundman, Richard J. "Will Diversion Reduce Recidivism?" *Crime and Delinquency* (October, 1976), p. 435.

36. Ibid., p. 436.

37. Shur. op. cit., p. 16.

38. McDermott. op. cit., pp. 2–3.

39. Ibid., p. 5.

40. Ibid., p. 12.

41. Ibid., p. 13.
42. Ibid., p. 14–15.
43. Ibid., p. 36.
44. Cressey. op. cit., p. 14.
45. Ibid., p. 2.
46. McDermott. op. cit., p. 28.
47. Cressey. op. cit., p. 4.
48. McDermott. op. cit., pp. 28–29.
49. Cressey. op. cit., pp. 12–13.
50. McDermott. op. cit., p. 29.
51. Ibid., pp. 20–30.
52. Ibid., p. 31.
53. Cressey. op. cit., pp. 32–33.
54. Ibid., p. 59.
55. Ibid., p. 62.
56. McDermott. op. cit., p. 5.
57. *Crime and Delinquency* (October, 1976). op. cit., p. 394.
58. McDermott. op. cit., pp. 7–9.
59. Ibid., pp. 9–10.
60. Ibid., pp. 10–11.
61. Blake, G. F. & Gibbons, D. "Evaluating the Impact of Juvenile Diversion Programs." *Crime and Delinquency* (October, 1976), p. 420.
62. Department of the California Youth Authority. *Youth Service Bureaus: A National Study*. Washington. Department of Health, Education and Welfare, 1972, p. 129.
63. Klein, Malcolm W. & Teilmann, K. *Pivotal Ingredients of Police Juvenile Diversion Programs*. Washington: Law Enforcement Assistance Administration, 1976, p. iv.
64. Cressey. op. cit., pp. 8–9.
65. Ibid., p. 59.
66. U.S. Department of Justice, National Institute of Law Enforcement and Criminal Justice. *Juvenile Diversion Through Family Counseling*. Washington: U.S. Government Printing Office, 1976, p. 8.
67. Ibid.
68. McSwain, Elwyn. *The Mecklenburg Youth Services Bureau: A Report on Progress Made Toward the Achievement of Measurable Goals and Objectives*. Charlotte, N.C.: Mecklenburg Youth Services Bureau, 1977, p. 3.

69. Ibid., pp. 17–18.

70. Heasley, C. Wayne. "Substitutes Rather Than Supplements to the Juvenile Justice System." *Prevention Profiles*. Richmond, Va.: Virginia Department of Corrections, Summer, 1977, pp. 3–5.

71. U.S. Department of Justice, National Institute of Law Enforcement and Criminal Justice. *The Philadelphia Neighborhood Youth Resources Center*. Washington: U.S. Government Printing Office, 1973.

71a. Ibid., p. 5.

72. U.S. Department of Justice, National Institute of Law Enforcement and Criminal Justice. *The Adolescent Diversion Project: A University's Approach to Delinquency Prevention*. Washington: U.S. Government Printing Office, 1977.

72a. Ibid., p. 7.

73. Ibid., pp. 6–9.

74. McDermott. op. cit., p. 26.

75. Ibid.

76. Ibid.

77. Cressey. op. cit., p. 4.

78. Hasenfeld. op. cit., p. 217.

79. Ibid., p. 71.

80. Ibid., p. 213.

81. Figlio, Robert M., Sellin, Thorsten, & Wolfgang, Marvin E. *Delinquency in a Birth Cohort*. Chicago: University of Chicago Press, 1972.

81a. Ibid., p. 68.

82. Ibid., p. 254.

83. Ibid., p. 248.

84. Ibid., p. 252.

85. Ibid., p. 251.

86. Ibid., p. 254.

87. Ibid., p. 251.

88. Ibid., p. 252.

89. Ibid.

90. National Association of Counties Research Foundation. *Juvenile Delinquency: A Basic Manual for County Officials*. Washington: National Association of Counties Research Foundation, 1976, p. 2.

91. Figlio et al. op. cit., p. 251.

92. Nettler, Gwynn. *Explaining Crime*. New York, Mcgraw-Hill Book Co., 1974, p. 76 in U.S. Department of Justice, *Program Announcement: Diversion of Youth from the Juvenile Justice System*, Op. Cit., p. 17.

93. Wilson, James Q. "The Police and the Delinquent in Two Cities," in Stanton Wheeler, ed., *Controlling Delinquents*. New York: John Wiley, 1968, pp. 9–30. Bordua, David J. "Recent Trends: Deviant Behavior and Social Control," *Annals of the American Academy of Political and Social Science* 359 (January 1967):149–61 in U.S. Department of Justice, *Program Announcement: Diversion of Youth from the Juvenile Justice System*, Op. Cit., p. 18–19.

94. Hohenstein, William F. "Factors Influencing the Police Disposition of Juvenile Offenders," in Thorsten Sellin and Marvin E. Wolfgang, eds., *Delinquency: Selected Studies*. New York: John Wiley, 1969, pp. 138–49. Sellin, Thorsten and Marvin E. Wolfgang. *The Measurement of Delinquency*. New York: John Wiley, 1964. Piliavin, Irving and Scott Briar. "Police Encounters with Juveniles," *American Journal of Sociology*. 70 (September 1964):206–214. Werthman, Carl and Irving Piliavin. "Gang Members and the Police," in David J. Bordua, ed., *The Police*. New York: John Wiley, 1967, in U.S. Department of Justice, *Program Announcement: Diversion of Youth*, Op. Cit., p. 19.

95. Cressey. Op. Cit., pp. 12–13.

96. Emerson, Robert M. *Judging Delinquents*. Chicago, Aldine Publishing Co., 1969, in U.S. Department of Justice *Program Announcement: Diversion of Youth from the Juvenile Justice System*, Op. Cit., p. 10.

97. Cressey. op. cit., pp. 12–13.

98. McDermott. op. cit., p. 39.

98a. Shur. op. cit., p. 155.

99. Cressey. op. cit., pp. 32–33.

100. Ibid., p. 59.

101. Ibid., p. 62.

102. McDermott. op. cit., p. 55.

103. Figlio et al. op. cit., p. 252.

104. Vinter, Robert D. (ed.). *Time Out: A National Study of Juvenile Correctional Programs*. Ann Arbor: National Assessment of Juvenile Corrections, University of Michigan, 1976, pp. 183–184.

105. Stumphauzer. op. cit., pp. 83–84.

106. *Crime and Delinquency* (October, 1976). op. cit., p. 412.

107. Department of the California Youth Authority. op. cit., p. 136.

CHAPTER 5

1. U.S. Department of Justice, Law Enforcement Assistance Administration, National Criminal Justice Information and Statistical Service. *Children in Custody: A Report on the Juvenile Detention and Correctional Facility Census of 1973.* Washington: U.S. Government Printing Office, 1977, p. 7.

2. Ibid., p. 5.

3. Vinter, Robert D., Downs, George, & Hall, John. *Juvenile Corrections in the States: Residential Programs and Deinstitutionalization.* Ann Arbor, Mich.: Institute of Continuing Legal Education, National Assessment of Legal Education, University of Michigan, 1976, pp. 28–29.

4. U.S. Department of Justice. op. cit., p. 5.

5. Ibid., p. 14.

6. Ibid.

7. Ibid., pp. 14, 21.

8. Ibid., p. 8.

9. Vinter et al. op. cit., p. 17.

10. Ibid., p. 18.

11. U.S. Department of Justice. op. cit., p. 31.

12. Vinter et al. op. cit., p. 25.

13. Goffman, Erving. *Asylums.* Chicago: Aldine Publishing Co., 1961, 386 pages.

14. Ibid., p. xiii.

15. Ibid., pp. 11–13.

16. Ibid., p. 15.

17. Ibid., p. 21.

18. Ibid., pp. 60–64.

19. Sykes, G. *The Society of Captives.* Princeton: Princeton University Press, 1958, 144 pages.

20. Ibid., p. 16.

21. Ibid., pp. 68–76.

22. Ibid., p. 17.

23. Ibid., p. 38.

24. Street D., Vinter, R. D. & Perrow, Charles. *Organization for Treatment: A*

Comparative Study of Institutions for Delinquents. New York: Free Press, 1966, p. 5.

25. Ibid., p. vii.

26. Ibid., pp. 21–25.

27. Ibid., p. 249.

28. Ibid., p. 251.

29. President's Commission on Law Enforcement and Administration of Justice. *The Challenge of Crime in a Free Society*. Washington: Government Printing Office, 1967, p. vii.

30. National Advisory Commission on Criminal Justice Standards and Goals. *A National Strategy to Reduce Crime*. Washington: U.S. Government Printing Office, 1973, p. 121.

31. U.S. Congress. *Public Law 93-415*, 1974.

32. Vinter et al. op. cit., passim pp. 40–46.

33. Ibid., p. 59.

34. Ibid., p. 61.

35. McCorkle, L. W., Elias, A., & Bixby, F. L. *The Highfields Story*. New York: Henry Holt and Co., 1958, 182 pages.

36. Empey, L. T. & Lubeck, S. G. *The Silverlake Experiment*. Chicago: Aldine Publishing Co., 1971, 354 pages.

37. Ibid., p. 15.

38. Ibid., pp. 16–17.

39. Ibid., p. 307.

40. Empey, L. T. & Erickson, M. E. *The Provo Experiment*. Chicago: Lexington Books, 1972, 321 pages.

41. Ibid., p. 10.

42. Ibid., p. 83.

43. Ibid., p. 89.

44. Ohlin, Lloyd E., Miller, Alden D., & Coates, Robert B. *Juvenile Correctional Reform in Massachusetts*. Washington: U.S. Department of Justice, Law Enforcement Assistance Administration, National Institute for Juvenile Justice and Delinquency Prevention, U.S. Government Printing Office, 1977, 116 pages.

45. Edelson, M. *Sociotherapy and Psychotherapy*. Chicago: University of Chicago Press, 1970, p. 179. Maxwell Jones et al. *The Therapeutic Community*, New York: Basic books, 1953.

46. *Juvenile Correctional Reform in Massachusetts*, op. cit., p. 28.

47. Ibid., introductory pages.

48. Ibid., introductory pages.

49. McEwen, C. A. *Designing Correctional Organizations for Youths: Dilemmas of Subcultural Development*. Cambridge, Mass.: Ballinger Publishing Co., 1978, p. 197.

50. Palmer, T., The Youth Authority's Community Treatment Project, *Federal Probation, 38*(1), 1974, pp. 3–14.

51. Ibid., p. 12.

52. President's Commission on Law Enforcement and Administration of Justice, op. cit., p. 81.

CHAPTER 6

1. Hasenfeld, Y. & Sarri, Rosemary C. (eds.). *Brought to Justice? Juveniles, the Courts and the Law*. Ann Arbor, Mich.: National Assessment of Juvenile Corrections, University of Michigan, 1976, pp. 180–181.

2. Ibid., p. 181.

3. Paulsen, M. B. & Whitebread, C. *Juvenile Law and Procedure*. Reno, Nev.: National Council of Juvenile Court Judges, 1974, pp. 12–13.

4. Ibid., pp. 15–16.

5. Ibid., p. 20.

6. Ibid.

7. Ibid., pp. 20–21.

8. National Juvenile Law Center, *Law and Tactics in Juvenile Cases*. St. Louis: St. Louis University School of Law, 1974, p. 11.

9. Hasenfeld. op. cit., p. 180.

10. Ibid., pp. 194–197.

11. Paulsen. op. cit., p. 183.

12. Ibid., p. 193.

13. LaPook, J. & Nejelski, Paul. "Monitoring the Juvenile Justice System: How Can You Tell Where You Are Going if You Don't Know Where You Are? *The American Criminal Law Review*. Washington: American Bar Association Section of Criminal Justice, Summer, 1974, p. 19.

14. Hasenfeld. op. cit., pp. 183–184.

15. Levin, M. M. & Sarri, Rosemary C. *Juvenile Delinquency: A Comparative Analysis of Legal Codes in the United States*. Ann Arbor, Mich.: National Assessment of Juvenile Corrections, University of Michigan, 1974, p. 38.

16. Hasenfeld. op. cit., p. 183.

17. Ibid.

18. Task Force on Juvenile Delinquency, The President's Crime Commission on Law Enforcement and the Administration of Justice. *Juvenile Delinquency and Youth Crime*. Washington: U.S. Government Printing Office, 1967, p. 40.

19. Paulsen. op. cit., p. 190.

20. Hasenfeld. op. cit., p. 186.

21. Ibid., pp. 184–185.

22. Ibid., p. 185.

23. Ibid., p. 186.

24. Paulsen, op. cit., p. 134.

25. Hasenfeld. op. cit., p. 188.

26. National Juvenile Law Center, *Law and Tactics in Juvenile Cases*. op. cit., p. 252.

27. Ibid., pp. 251–252.

28. Hasenfeld. op. cit., p. 188.

29. National Juvenile Law Center, *Law and Tactics in Juvenile Cases*. op. cit., pp. 113–114.

30. Ibid., p. 117.

31. Hasenfeld. op. cit., pp. 189–190.

32. Ibid., p. 189.

33. Paulsen. op. cit., p. 114.

34. Hasenfeld. op. cit., p. 189.

35. Levin. op. cit., pp. 53–54.

36. Hasenfeld. op. cit., p. 191.

37. Ibid.

38. Levin. op. cit., p. 49.

39. Hasenfeld, op. cit., p. 191.

40. Davis, Samuel M. *Rights of Juveniles: The Juvenile Justice System*. New York: Clark Boardman Company, Ltd., 1974, p. 126.

41. Levin, op. cit., pp. 50–51.

42. Davis. op. cit., p. 126–129.

43. Hasenfeld. op. cit., pp. 191–192.

44. Ibid., p. 192.

45. Ibid., p. 196.

46. Ibid.

47. Ibid., p. 192.

48. Ibid., pp. 192–194.

49. Duffee, D. and Larry Siegel, "The Organization Man: Legal Counsel in the Juvenile Court," Brantingham, P. & Faust, F. (eds.) *Juvenile Justice Philosophy: Readings, Cases, Comments.* St. Paul: West Publishing Company, 1974, pp. 498–499.

50. Ibid., p. 506.

51. Lefstein, N., Vaughn Stapleton and Lee Teitelbaum, "In Search of Juvenile Justice: Gault and Its Implementation," *Criminal Law in Action.* Chambless, William J. (ed.) Santa Barbara, California: Hamilton Publishing Company, 1975, pp. 386–392.

52. Hasenfeld. op. cit., p. 198.

53. Ibid., pp. 199–200.

54. Rubin, H. Ted. "The Juvenile Court's Search for Identity and Responsibility." *Crime and Delinquency* (January, 1977), p. 12.

CHAPTER 7

1. Gibbons, Don C. *Society, Crime and Criminal Careers: An Introduction to Criminology.* Englewood Cliffs, N.J.: Prentice-Hall, Inc., 1977, p. 97.

2. Perrow, Charles. *Organizational Analysis: A Sociological View.* Belmont: Wadsworth Publishing Co., 1970, p. 128.

3. Center for Action Research, Inc. *A Design for Youth Development Policy.* Boulder, Colorado: Center for Action Research, Inc., 1976, p. 174.

4. Lemert, Edwin M. *Instead of Court: Diversion in Juvenile Justice.* Washington: U.S. Government Printing Office, 1971, p. 82.

5. Ibid., p. 91.

6. Hasenfeld, Y. & Sarri, R. (eds.) *Brought to Justice? Juveniles, the Courts and the Law.* Ann Arbor, Mich.: National Assessment of Juvenile Corrections, University of Michigan, 1976, pp. 67–68.

7. Ibid., p. 63.

8. Ibid., p. 91.

9. Ibid., p. 88.

10. Ibid., pp. 91–95.

11. Ibid., p. 95.

12. Ibid., pp. 72–74.

13. Center for Action Research, Inc. op. cit., p. 173.

14. Hasenfeld. op. cit., p. 67.

15. Ibid., pp. 69–71.

16. Ibid., p. 162.

17. Downs, George, Hall, John, & Vinter, Robert D. *Juvenile Corrections in the States: Residential Programs and Deinstitutionalization.* Ann Arbor, Mich.: National Assessment of Juvenile Corrections, University of Michigan, 1976, p. 66.

18. Ibid., p. 73.   •

19. Hasenfeld. op. cit., p. 165.

INDEX